NORWICH CITY COLLEGE LIBRARY

Stock No.	190780	
Class	541.042	
Cat.		Proc.	QS

Gases, Liquids and Solids

Philip Matthews

Series editor: Brian Ratcliff

CAMBRIDGE
UNIVERSITY

190 780

PUBLISHED BY THE PRESS SYNDICATE OF THE UNIVERSITY OF CAMBRIDGE
The Pitt Building, Trumpington Street, Cambridge, United Kingdom

CAMBRIDGE UNIVERSITY PRESS
The Edinburgh Building, Cambridge CB2 2RU, UK
40 West 20th Street, New York, NY 10011–4211, USA
477 Williamstown Road, Port Melbourne, VIC 3207, Australia
Ruiz de Alarcón 13, 28014 Madrid, Spain
Dock House, The Waterfront, Cape Town 8001, South Africa

http://www.cambridge.org

© Cambridge University Press 2002

First published 2002

Printed in the United Kingdom at the University Press, Cambridge

Typeface Swift   *System* QuarkXPress®

A catalogue record for this book is available from the British Library

ISBN 0 521 79750 0 paperback

Produced by Gecko Ltd, Bicester, Oxon

Front cover photograph: Lava flowing from erupting volcano, Hawaii Island,
Hawaii, USA; Tony Stone Images Ltd.

NOTICE TO TEACHERS
It is illegal to reproduce any part of this work in material form (including
photocopying and electronic storage) except under the following circumstances:
(i)   where you are abiding by a licence granted to your school or institution by
       the Copyright Licensing Agency;
(ii)   where no such licence exists, or where you wish to exceed the terms of a
       licence, and you have gained the written permission of Cambridge
       University Press;
(iii) where you are allowed to reproduce without permission under the
       provisions of Chapter 3 of the Copyright, Designs and Patents Act 1988.

Contents

Introduction

Cambridge Advanced Sciences

The *Cambridge Advanced Sciences* series has been developed to meet the demands of all the new AS and A level science examinations. In particular, it has been endorsed by OCR as providing complete coverage of their specifications. The AS material is presented as a single text for each of biology, chemistry and physics. Material for the A2 year comprises six books in each subject: one of core material and one for each option. Some material has been drawn from the existing *Cambridge Modular Sciences* books; however, the majority is entirely new.

During the development of this series, the opportunity has been taken to improve the design, and a complete and thorough new writing and editing process has been applied. Much more material is now presented in colour. Although the existing *Cambridge Modular Sciences* texts do cover some of the new specifications, the *Cambridge Advanced Sciences* books cover every OCR learning objective in detail. They are the key to success in the new AS and A level examinations.

OCR is one of the three unitary awarding bodies offering the full range of academic and vocational qualifications in the UK. For full details of the new specifications, please contact OCR:

OCR, 1 Hills Rd, Cambridge CB1 2EU
Tel: 01223 553311   http://www.ocr.org.uk

The presentation of units

You will find that the books in this series use a bracketed convention in the presentation of units within tables and on graph axes. For example, ionisation energies of $1000\,kJ\,mol^{-1}$ and $2000\,kJ\,mol^{-1}$ will be represented in this way:

Measurement	Ionisation energy ($kJ\,mol^{-1}$)
1	1000
2	2000

OCR examination papers use the solidus as a convention, thus:

Measurement	Ionisation energy / $kJ\,mol^{-1}$
1	1000
2	2000

Any numbers appearing in brackets with the units, for example $(10^{-5}\,mol\,dm^{-3}\,s^{-1})$, should be treated in exactly the same way as when preceded by the solidus, $/10^{-5}\,mol\,dm^{-3}\,s^{-1}$.

Gases, Liquids and Solids – an A2 option text

Gases, Liquids and Solids contains everything needed to cover the A2 option of the same name. It is a brand new text which has been written specifically with the new OCR specification in mind. A specialised glossary of terms is included, linked to the main text via the index.

The book is divided into four chapters corresponding to the module sections States of Matter, Phase Diagrams, Distribution Between Phases, and Raoult's Law and Distillation.

The module builds upon material in *Chemistry 1*, in particular aspects of Structure and Bonding from the Foundation Chemistry module. Please note that some prior knowledge required to cover this module is not covered until the synoptic unit of the A2 course. However, supporting material can be found in *Chemistry 2*.

Acknowledgements

1.1a,b,c, USGS; 1.6, Stefan Lesiansky/University of Leeds; 1.7 Press Association; 1.9, Bryan and Cherry Alexander; 1.15, John Cleare; 1.17, 2.1a,b,c, 3.3, 4.9, Andrew Lambert; 1.19, Barbara Berkowitz/Life File; 1.22, Jan Suttle/Life File; 2.4, Andrew Pine/ Cambridge University Press; 2.5, Andrew Putler/ Redferns; 2.11, TEK Image/Science Photo Library; 2.20, 3.2, ATM Images; 3.1, Robert Harding; 3.5, Kieran Murray/Ecoscene; 3.7, Neil Thompson; 3.8, Bubbles/Ian West; 4.1t, b, Robert Harding Picture Library; 4.8, Nigel Luckhurst

Every effort has been made to contact copyright holders; Cambridge University Press would be happy to hear from anyone whose rights have been unwittingly infringed.

CHAPTER 1

States of matter

By the end of this chapter you should be able to:

1 describe, using a *kinetic–molecular model*, the solid, liquid and gaseous states, melting, vaporisation and vapour pressure;

2 state the basic assumptions of the *kinetic theory* as applied to an ideal gas;

3 explain qualitatively, in terms of *intermolecular forces* and *molecular size*, (i) the conditions necessary for a gas to approach *ideal behaviour*, and (ii) the *limitations of ideality* at very high pressures and very low temperatures;

4 state and use the *ideal gas equation PV = nRT* in calculations, including the determination of the relative molecular mass of a volatile liquid.

The three states of matter

Figure 1.1 shows the Grinnell glacier, at various times in the past. You can see just how much of the glacier has disappeared between 1914 and 1997. Many scientists believe that the increasing rate of melting of glacier ice, and ice at the polar ice caps, is a result of global warming. You may know that, if global warming continues, the sea level on Earth will gradually rise. Mainly the rise will be due to the expansion of sea water; but the melt water from glaciers and the polar ice caps will add to the increase as well. In fact, it has been estimated that, if all the ice over the Earth's land mass were to melt, sea level would rise by around 20 m. For many Europeans, the retreat of glaciers in mountainous regions and the end of reliable winter snow falls will be the end of skiing holidays. However, there are far more serious consequences world wide; for example, glaciers provide billions of gallons of water for drinking water and the irrigation of crops in lowland regions. In Africa, the end of glaciation will make vast tracts of land uninhabitable owing to the lack of melt water. It has been estimated that a rise of 4 °C in average air temperature will be enough to melt all the glaciers in Europe, and even the Himalayas.

Studying the conditions that cause ice to form, and melt, and the change of water vapour into

● **Figure 1.1** Three photographs of the Grinnell glacier, Glacier National Park, USA, taken in **a** 1914, **b** 1938 and **c** 1997.

rain and snow, is part of chemistry. We know how and why water changes between its solid, liquid and gaseous forms; and this knowledge is important in predicting the results of global warming. However, the same processes are at work when any solid, liquid or gas changes from one form to another. This book will introduce you to the main factors that we believe are responsible for the different properties of gases, liquids and solids. However, as in all good stories, we should start at the beginning; and that means you need to know what we mean by states of matter.

The three **states of matter** are solid, liquid and gas. Whether a substance exists as a solid, liquid or gas mainly depends on two things:

1 *Kinetic energy* – which increases as a substance is heated.
2 *Intermolecular forces* – the forces between the molecules that make up the substance.

The kinetic energy of the molecules in a solid, liquid or gas is a measure of the amount of random movement of molecules. The more kinetic energy the molecules of a substance have, the greater is the tendency for its molecules to be jumbled up, i.e. to be more disordered. The most *disorderly* arrangement that molecules can achieve is in a gas. At the other extreme, the most orderly arrangement is in a solid. Liquids are somewhere in between. See *figure 1.2*.

Intermolecular forces tend to hold molecules together. There are intermolecular forces between all molecules; but between some they are very weak, and between others they are quite strong. When the forces are weak, the molecules are not likely to cling together to make a liquid or solid unless they have very little kinetic energy. The

noble gases are excellent examples of this. For instance, helium will not liquefy until the temperature is almost as low as −269 °C, or 4 K. On the other hand, the intermolecular forces between water molecules are very strong – strong enough to hold them together up to 100 °C.

To summarise, we can say that:

> Intermolecular forces tend to bring order to the movements of molecules.
> Kinetic energy brings disorder, and leads in the direction of randomness or chaos.

Thus, at a given temperature, a substance will exist as a solid, liquid or gas depending on where the balance between these two opposing influences lies. We saw in *Chemistry 1*, chapter 15, and shall see on page 8 in this book, that an *equilibrium* can be set up when a substance changes state.

How do we know that gases are disorderly?

One piece of evidence for this comes indirectly from the experiments first performed by Robert Brown in 1827. He observed the movement of pollen on the surface of water, which he found to be completely unpredictable. The random movements of the pollen, known as **Brownian motion**, were finally given a mathematical explanation by Albert Einstein (of relativity fame) in 1905. He showed that a grain of pollen went on a random walk. **a random walk** (*figure 1.3*) is the sort of walk that a very drunk person would go on if put out in an open space. If we assume that the drunk found it impossible to make a conscious choice, he (or she) would be as likely to walk in one direction as any other. The reason why the grains

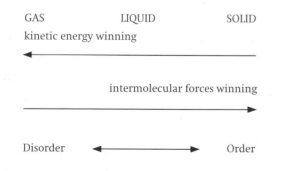

GAS   LIQUID   SOLID
kinetic energy winning

intermolecular forces winning

Disorder ⟷ Order

● **Figure 1.2** The relation between kinetic energy, disorder and intermolecular forces.

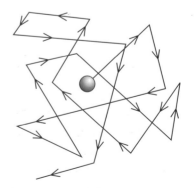

● **Figure 1.3** A random walk of a pollen grain.

behave in this way is that they are being bombarded by molecules in the liquid, which are themselves moving in a random way.

Around 1908 Jean Perrin made observations of Brownian motion in gases. He showed that small particles, much larger than individual molecules but still very small (less than 10^{-6} m in diameter), also went on random walks. This could only be explained along the same lines as Brownian motion in liquids. The particles were being struck by the randomly moving gas molecules.

How much order is there in a liquid?

The particles in a liquid group together, and it is just this tendency that produces some order in their arrangement (*figure 1.4*). However, the order is over a relatively short range, perhaps over a distance of 10^{-9} m (about 10 molecular diameters). Over greater distances, the degree of order diminishes, i.e. the groups themselves are randomly arranged. We can summarise the situation in this way:

In a liquid there is short-range order, and long-range disorder.

However, as in a gas, the positions of the particles in a liquid are constantly changing; so membership of the groups is always changing.

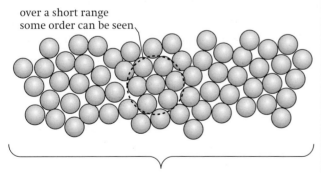

over a short range some order can be seen

over a long range there is little order

● **Figure 1.4** Order and disorder in a liquid.

The arrangement of particles in a solid

First, a reminder: there are many types of solid, whose properties depend on the particles that they contain. For example, metal crystals consist of lattices of atoms, which are best viewed as positive ions existing in a 'sea' of electrons; ionic

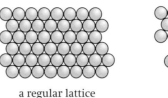
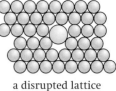

a regular lattice   a disrupted lattice with an impurity atom

● **Figure 1.5** Disorder can appear even in very orderly solids.

substances like sodium chloride have lattices built from positively and negatively charged ions (Na^+ and Cl^-); iodine crystals have a lattice of iodine molecules, I_2; graphite crystals contain layers of hexagonal rings of carbon atoms; and diamond is a giant lattice of carbon atoms all bonded in a tetrahedral arrangement. In general, metals and ionic substances have high melting points (although there are exceptions); molecular crystals (like iodine) have low melting points; and giant lattices of interlocked atoms (like diamond) have very high melting points. For the sake of keeping our description of solids fairly simple, we shall use metal crystals as our examples of solids. Much of what we shall say about the structures of metals applies to other types of solids (and when it doesn't, we shall say why).

When a liquid metal starts to crystallise, the atoms begin to fit together in regular patterns. A particularly simple pattern is shown in *figure 1.5*. It is clear that this is a very orderly arrangement. However, even at 0 K, the atoms are not completely still; they vibrate about the same average position. The very regular packing of particles in a solid extends over far greater distances than in a liquid. However, eventually the regularity breaks down. This can happen because of impurity atoms getting in the way, and blocking the normal pattern. It can also happen when crystals start to grow in several places and grow towards each other. Where the crystalline regions meet, the two lattices may not meet exactly. We can visualise such situations in the laboratory using bubble rafts, like that in *figure 1.6*. The study of order and disorder in metal crystals is of huge importance in industry. Variations in a metal lattice can lead to greater strength or, more worryingly, to metal fatigue (*figure 1.7*).

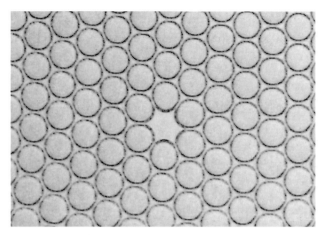

● **Figure 1.6** Bubble rafts can be used to show perfect order and imperfections.

● **Figure 1.7** Metal fatigue in the rails is likely to have contributed to the October 2000 Hatfield train crash.

Differences in properties of solids, liquids and gases

As we have seen, the particles in a gas are, on average, much further apart than they are in a liquid or solid (*figure 1.8*). There is very little difference

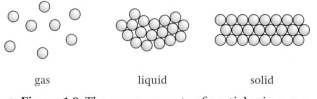

gas   liquid   solid

● **Figure 1.8** The arrangements of particles in a gas, a liquid and a solid.

between the spacing of atoms in liquids and solids; that is why both liquids and solids are hard to compress. Also, the particles in a gas travel very much faster than those in a liquid. The differences in spacing, and in speed, are the main reason for the different properties of the three states of matter (*figure 1.9* and *table 1.1*). For example, notice that gases are not very good conductors of heat. For heat to be conducted by atoms or molecules, the movement energy of the molecules must be

● **Figure 1.9** Cloud, sea and iceberg – the three states of matter.

	Solids	**Liquids**	**Gases**
Amount of order of arrangement of particles	Very orderly	Short-range order, longer-range disorder	Almost complete disorder
Shape	Fixed	Takes shape of container	No shape
Position of particles	Fixed; no movement from place to place	Some movement from place to place	Always moving rapidly from place to place
Spacing of particles	Close ($\approx 10^{-10}$ m)	Close ($\approx 10^{-10}$ m)	Far apart ($\approx 10^{-8}$ m)
Compressibility	Very low	Very low	High
Conduction of heat	Metals and graphite very good; others poor	Metals very good; others poor	Very poor

● **Table 1.1** Comparison of properties of the three states of matter.

passed on from one to another. This requires the molecules to collide, which happens less easily in a gas than in a liquid.

In a solid the particles are held in position by the overall effects of the attractions and repulsions of their neighbours. Even so, the particles do have some movement. They vibrate to and fro, although on average they keep the same position. As the temperature increases, they vibrate more violently, and they pass on the energy of their vibrations to their neighbours. However, the only solids that conduct heat very well are those that have electrons that can move from place to place. Especially, metals have many **free electrons** that can carry their movement energy with them even though the ions themselves are stuck in one place. That is, metals conduct heat well because of their free electrons, not as a result of vibrations of the particles.

Owing to the large amount of empty space in a gas, it is fairly easy to squeeze the molecules into a smaller volume; so gases are easily compressed.

Liquids and solids have their molecules already very close together, so they are very difficult to compress.

Comparing the melting and boiling points of substances

You will find some representative examples of melting and boiling points in *table 1.2*. A column showing the relative molecular masses (M_r) of the molecules has been included in the table. If you look carefully, you will see that there is a *general* rule that governs the values:

> The higher the relative molecular mass, the higher the melting point and the higher the boiling point.

One reason why melting and boiling points tend to increase with mass is that, the greater the mass of a molecule, the more electrons it

	Relative molecular mass, M_r	Melting pt (°C)	Boiling pt (°C)		Relative molecular mass, M_r	Melting pt (°C)	Boiling pt (°C)
Elements				*Compounds*			
Helium, He	4		−269	Methane, CH_4	16	−182	−161
Neon, Ne	20	−249	−249	Ethane, C_2H_6	30	−183	−88
Argon, Ar	37	−189	−186	Propane, C_3H_8	44	−189	−42
Krypton, Kr	84	−157	−152	Butane, C_4H_{10}	58	−138	0
Fluorine, F_2	38	−220	−188	Methanol, CH_3OH	32	−98	65
Chlorine, Cl_2	71	−101	−34	Ethanol, C_2H_5OH	46	−68	79
Bromine, Br_2	160	−7	58	Propan-1-ol, C_3H_7OH	60	−78	97
Iodine, I_2	230	114	183	Butan-1-ol, C_4H_9OH	74	−89	118
Carbon (diamond), C	12	3550	4830	Hydrogen fluoride, HF	20	−83	20
Silicon, Si	28	1410	2680	Hydrogen chloride, HCl	36.5	−114	−85
Germanium, Ge	73	940	2830	Hydrogen bromide, HBr	81	−87	−67
Tin (white), Sn	119	232	2690	Hydrogen iodide, HI	116	−51	−35
Oxygen, O_2	32	−219	−183	Water, H_2O	18	0	100
Sulphur, S	32	114.5	444.6	Hydrogen sulphide, H_2S	34	−85	−60
Selenium, Se	79	217	685	Hydrogen selenide, H_2Se	81	−66	−42
Tellurium, Te	128	450	1390	Hydrogen telluride, H_2Te	130	−49	−2

● **Table 1.2** Melting points and boiling points of some elements and compounds.
  (Values have been measured at standard atmospheric pressure, 100 kPa.)

possesses. It is one of the features of large molecules that their electron clouds are more spread out (diffuse), and it is just this type of molecule that has large forces between instantaneous dipoles. These forces are called **instantaneous dipole forces** (more correctly 'instantaneous dipole-induced dipole forces', and are also known as **van der Waals' forces**). Thus, as molecules get heavier, the instantaneous dipole forces become greater, and tend to keep the molecules together.

However, there are many exceptions to the general rule. In particular, you should know that:

> Where melting or boiling points are higher than expected, look for very strong intermolecular forces at work, especially hydrogen bonds.

There are two important examples that you should know about:

■ *Hydrogen fluoride*, HF, is rather like water in that its boiling point is far above those of the other hydrides of the halogens. The reason is, again, *hydrogen bonding*. Fluorine is the most electronegative of all the elements, and the hydrogen fluoride molecule is extremely polar. That is, the fluorine atom attracts the pair of electrons in the H–F bond towards itself. The bonding pair spend most of the time nearer the fluorine, thus giving the atom an excess of negative charge. The hydrogen atom has its nucleus (a single proton) only partially surrounded by electrons, and therefore it has an excess positive charge. We show the slight positive and negative charges by the symbols δ+ ('delta-plus') and δ– ('delta-minus'). The hydrogen bonds are the forces of attraction between the opposite charges and are shown by the dotted lines in *figure 1.10*.

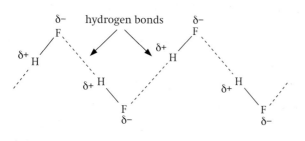

● **Figure 1.10** A representation of the structure of solid hydrogen fluoride, where the molecules take up a zig-zag shape. The molecules are held together by hydrogen bonds.

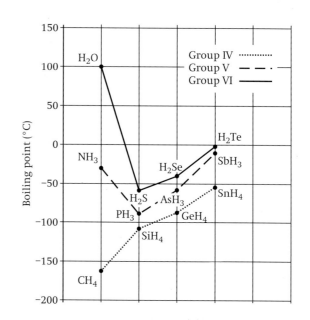

● **Figure 1.11** The boiling points of the Group IV, V and VI hydrides.

■ *The Group VI hydrides*, especially water, H_2O. Compared to the other hydrides of Group VI, the melting and boiling points of water are remarkably high. (The values are shown in *table 1.2*, and a graph of the data is included in *figure 1.11*.) The reason for this lies in hydrogen bonding (*figure 1.12*). In every one of its states, water molecules can hydrogen bond together. In ice the regular arrangement of the lattice leaves a large amount of free space. *Figure 1.13* illustrates the extent of the free space. Because the water molecules in ice are not so close together as in liquid water, ice is less dense than liquid water. In liquid water there is a tremendous amount of order compared to other liquids. Although the pattern of hydrogen bonding is always changing, water molecules are held together much more tightly than are molecules in most other liquids.

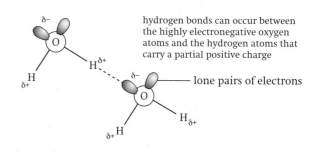

● **Figure 1.12** The origin of hydrogen bonding in water.

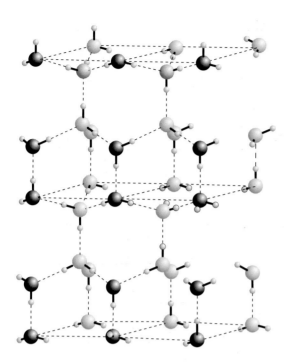

● **Figure 1.13** The structure of ice.

SAQ 1.1

As shown in *figure 1.11*, water and ammonia have boiling points much higher than those of the other hydrides of the elements in their Groups. However, the boiling point of methane, CH_4, is lower than those of the other hydrides of Group IV. What is the reason for the difference?

Why gases liquefy, and solids melt

When two molecules are far apart, they move completely independently; neither will feel the presence of the other. However, if they come closer, then intermolecular forces get to work. The two molecules will attract one another. You will have learned about attractive intermolecular forces when you studied instantaneous dipole forces in *Chemistry 1*, chapter 3. Also, you should have come across hydrogen bonding and dipole–dipole interactions as intermolecular forces that tend to bring molecules together. However, think about molecules coming *very* close together. The 'outside' of a molecule is really a layer of negatively charged electrons: the **electron cloud**. When molecules

approach closely, the electron clouds repel one another. It is the great strength of the repulsion that puts a limit on how close the atoms can get.

If two molecules collide with a great deal of energy, the negatively charged electron clouds get squeezed together and the resulting repulsion pushes them apart. Indeed, in a gas the force is so great that it overcomes the (attractive) intermolecular forces. Thus the molecules return to their life of rushing round at random in the body of the gas.

On the other hand, at lower temperatures the speeds of the molecules are lower and the force of collisions can be much less. There is a better chance of the intermolecular forces equalling, and indeed being greater than, the repulsive forces as the molecules collide. When this happens the molecules will not spring apart. Rather, they will remain close together and we see the gas turning to a liquid.

The molecules of different gases have their own characteristic intermolecular forces, and repulsive forces between their electron clouds. Therefore the temperature at which the forces between colliding molecules become low enough for the instantaneous dipole forces to win is different for every gas; i.e. different gases liquefy at different temperatures.

We can turn this line of argument on its head, and explain the change of liquid to gas by discussing the two opposing forces as the temperature of a liquid increases to its boiling point (see SAQ 1.2).

SAQ 1.2

a Use your knowledge of intermolecular attractions and repulsions to explain why liquids turn into gases as the temperature increases.
b Why does every substance have its own particular boiling point?

Explaining changes of state

Everyone is familiar with the change of liquid water to a vapour. This happens when water evaporates from a puddle, or when washing dries on a windy or sunny day, or when water boils in a kettle. Likewise, most people in industrialised countries convert liquid water into a solid, ice, by cooling water in a freezer. To understand why, and how, a substance changes state you need to know about intermolecular forces that attract molecules to each other, and the repulsions between the electron clouds when molecules get very close together. However, you also need to understand two further ideas: the first is that of *equilibrium*, and the second is the idea of *vapour pressure*.

We can bring these together by thinking about an experiment to measure the vapour pressure of a liquid, illustrated in *figure 1.14*. (You are not expected to know the details of the experiment for your examinations.) The idea is to introduce a small quantity of the liquid into a tube filled with mercury. (Owing to the high density of mercury, the liquid will float to the top.) Without the liquid, there would be a vacuum above the mercury, and, at standard conditions, the column of mercury would be 760 mm tall. With the liquid present, some of the molecules escape into the space. Once in the vapour, they exert a pressure, and the mercury is pushed down slightly; i.e. the height of the mercury column is reduced. The difference between the heights (once some corrections are made for the presence of the liquid) is the vapour pressure of the liquid.

The molecules that escape from the surface of the liquid tend to have higher than average energies – that is why they escape. If a molecule has lower than, or about the same as, the average energy it is unlikely to escape the clutches of the other molecules – the intermolecular forces will hold it back. However, as more molecules escape into the space above the mercury, the chances of them bouncing back into the surface of the liquid increase. Eventually, the chance of a molecule leaving the surface equals the chance of a molecule in the vapour joining the liquid. At that time, **equilibrium** is reached (see *Chemistry 1*, page 180):

> At equilibrium, the rate at which molecules leave the liquid equals the rate at which molecules join the liquid.

At equilibrium, the space above the liquid has become saturated with the vapour – it contains the maximum amount of vapour possible at the given temperature. (If we were to increase the temperature of the apparatus, more vapour could exist in the space above the liquid, and the vapour pressure would increase.) Make sure you realise that equilibrium is a *dynamic* process: there is a great deal of change going on with molecules constantly leaving and joining the liquid. However, they do so at the same rate (many millions per second). *Figure 1.14* shows how evaporation of a liquid can take place under equilibrium conditions.

However, equilibrium will not always be achieved. For example, on a warm, windy day, wet clothes dry very quickly because the atmosphere is not saturated with water vapour as it would be on a cold, wet day. There are (relatively) so few water molecules in the atmosphere that they have little chance of going back on to the clothes once they have left the surface, or of water molecules already in the air sticking to the clothes. That is, wet clothes drying on a line will not reach equilibrium like the liquid in *figure 1.14*.

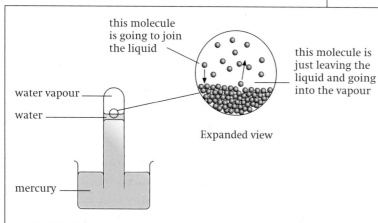

● **Figure 1.14** Measuring the vapour pressure of a liquid (note that the diagram is not to scale).

● **Figure 1.15** Water boiling under reduced pressure. Water will boil even at room temperature if the pressure is low enough.

If we heat a liquid we give more energy to the molecules. This increases their chance of leaving the surface, and the liquid will evaporate more quickly. If we continue to heat the liquid, it will eventually boil (*figure 1.15*). We shall not prove it, but the condition for a liquid to boil is that:

A liquid boils when its vapour pressure equals atmospheric pressure.

We shall return to this point later (see page 19).

SAQ 1.3

If you put a little alcohol (ethanol) or propanone on the back of your hand, the liquid will evaporate and you will feel the back of your hand get cold. Why does evaporation lead to cooling? [*Hint:* Think about the range of energies the molecules possess, and why even the less energetic particles eventually evaporate.]

SAQ 1.4

What are clouds made of? Briefly explain why clouds form, and why they often lead to rain falling.

Some remarkable substances

In this section we shall briefly consider some substances that are difficult to classify as a solid, liquid or gas.

Liquid crystals

It seems a contradiction to call a crystal 'liquid'. We expect crystals to be solids, and certainly not liquids. Essentially, **liquid crystals** are liquids that have sufficient long-range order in them to make them behave like a solid. However, they will only behave like a solid over a certain range of temperatures. Usually a liquid crystal is made from molecules that are long, thin and not very symmetrical. You will find some examples in *figure 1.16*.

The intermolecular forces must be strong enough to hold the molecules together, but not so strong as to restrict their movement too much. The unsymmetrical nature of the molecules leads

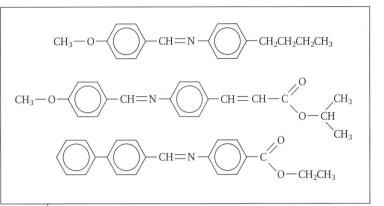

● **Figure 1.16** Examples of molecules that make liquid crystals.

to an unsymmetrical packing of the molecules. The very useful property of liquid crystals is that the arrangement of the molecules can be upset by very slight changes in their surroundings. Especially, in the liquid crystals used in calculators, digital watches and computer displays (*figure 1.17*), the molecules rearrange themselves when the crystal is subjected to a small electric field. The rearrangement changes the way the crystal absorbs light.

● **Figure 1.17** A liquid crystal display.

Glass

Glass is a most unusual material. For example, it allows light to pass through it very easily. Also, it melts over a range of temperatures and remains viscous (rather like treacle). This allows glass to be 'blown into many different shapes (*figure 1.19*), or to be rolled into sheets for use in windows. The basic building block of ordinary glass is a tetrahedron built from a silicon atom with four oxygen atoms around it (*figure 1.18* on page 10). The tetrahedra join to give a three-dimensional interlocking structure that gives glass its high

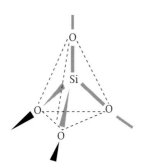

● **Figure 1.18** The tetrahedral group of a central silicon atom and four oxygen atoms that is the basis for the structure of glass.

viscosity. However, unlike a normal solid, glass has no long-range order in its structure.

In 1880 the Irish physicist John Tyndall (who had a 'professional interest' in ice, as he was an extremely keen mountaineer) compared ice and glass in this way: "The ice is music, the glass is noise – the ice is order, the glass is confusion. In the glass, molecular forces constitute an

● **Figure 1.19** A glass blower. Glass remains viscous over a large range of temperatures, which allows it to be blown into an amazing variety of shapes.

inextricably entangled skein, in the ice they are woven to a symmetric web." (Quoted in W. H. Brock et al., *John Tyndall*, Royal Dublin Society, 1981, page 98.)

Real and ideal gases

Now we shall consider the properties of gases in greater depth. To begin with, you need to know that gases show these properties:

1 They fill all the space open to them.
2 They expand when heated.
3 They exert a pressure on the walls of their containers.
4 The pressure changes as the temperature changes.

Shortly, we shall deal with each of these in more detail; but you will find that we shall spend only part of the time discussing the properties of real gases such as hydrogen, oxygen, methane and so on. Real gases are complicated things, and it can be helpful at first to use a simplified model of a gas. In fact, much of this unit will be about 'gases' that do not exist in the real world – these are gases that we call *ideal gases*.

The behaviour of ideal gases

Ideal gases have some, but not all, of the properties of real gases. A brief summary of the characteristics of an **ideal gas** is given in *box 1A*. An ideal gas is a gas in which there are no intermolecular forces, and in which the molecules don't take up any space themselves (we regard them as points). Also, we assume that the molecules do not change their total kinetic energy when they bump into each other; this is what we mean if we say that the collisions are 'perfectly elastic'. No real gas is ideal, although some come close to ideal behaviour, e.g. helium. You will find that we can compare real and ideal gases, and from their different characteristics we can learn a great deal about real gases. The key idea is to explain why real gases are different from ideal gases – but more of this later.

> **Box 1A Key assumptions about ideal gases**
> *In an ideal gas:*
> ■ the molecules have mass, but negligible size;
> ■ there are no intermolecular forces;
> ■ the collisions between the molecules are perfectly elastic.

The kinetic theory of gases

You will already know that the molecules in a gas are in a constant state of random motion. This feature of gases is one of the main foundations of the **kinetic theory of gases**. A statement of the main features of the kinetic theory of gases is given in *box 1B*. As far as we know, the kinetic theory of gases is an extremely well-supported theory. There is a great deal of evidence to show that, to all intents

Box 1B The kinetic theory of gases

Main idea:
■ Gases consist of molecules in a constant state of random motion.

Related ideas:
■ The pressure of a gas is due to the collisions of the molecules with the walls of the container.
■ The molecules travel in straight lines until they collide with one another, or with the walls of the container.
■ In these collisions, the total kinetic energy of the molecules does not change.

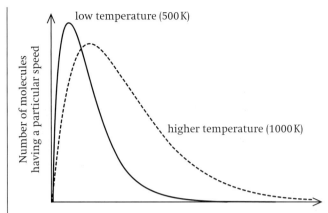

● **Figure 1.20** How the distribution of the kinetic energy of the molecules in a gas changes with temperature.

and purposes, the motion of gas molecules is random. This means that in any gas, on average, there will be as many molecules moving in one direction as in any other direction.

You might like to know that the average speed of gas molecules is of the order of $500\,\text{m s}^{-1}$ at room temperature. The lighter the molecule, the greater the average speed (and vice versa). For example, hydrogen molecules have an average speed somewhat above $1500\,\text{m s}^{-1}$, and carbon dioxide molecules have an average speed nearer to $350\,\text{m s}^{-1}$.

There is a wide range of energies among the molecules in a gas. Some move very rapidly, and much faster than the average, and some move very much more slowly than the average. When a gas is heated, *on average* all the molecules increase their kinetic energies (i.e. move faster); but this does not mean that they *all* increase. Always, some will pick up more energy than others. Indeed, during a collision between two molecules, one of them may move off with a greater speed, and one with a lower speed than before. However, the majority move near to the average speed. The way the kinetic energy of the molecules varies with temperature is shown in *figure 1.20*. As the temperature goes up, the average energy of all the molecules increases, but the distribution of speeds, and therefore kinetic energies, spreads out. Especially, the proportion of molecules with high kinetic energies increases. If you look carefully at the shapes of the graphs, you will see that they are not quite symmetrical – the curve stretches out more at higher than at lower energies. (This is an important point when explaining how changes in temperature influence the rates of chemical reactions: see *Chemistry 1*, page 169.)

SAQ 1.5

Use ideas from the kinetic theory of gases to answer these two questions:

a What happens to the average kinetic energy of the molecules in a gas as the temperature increases?

b What might happen to the kinetic energy of any individual molecule in a gas as the temperature increases?

The pressure and volume of an ideal gas

The pressure of a gas is caused by the collisions of the molecules with the walls of its container. By doing some mathematics, it is possible to show that the pressure of an ideal gas depends on three factors:

1 the number of molecules per unit volume (i.e. the concentration of the gas);
2 the mass of the molecules;
3 their speed.

This should make sense to you because, if there are more molecules present in a given volume, there should be more collisions with the walls, so the pressure should increase. Likewise, if the molecules have a greater momentum (mass times speed), the harder they will bounce off the walls. Therefore, they exert a greater force on the walls, and cause the pressure to increase.

SAQ 1.6

Look at *figure 1.21*. Two identical cylinders A and B fitted with pistons are kept in different rooms. Both contain the same number of molecules of gas, but the volume of one (A) is less than that of the other (B). What is the most likely reason for the difference in volume?

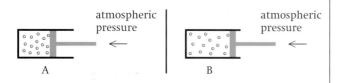

● **Figure 1.21** Both sets of cylinders and pistons A and B are subject to the same atmospheric pressure, and both contain the same number of molecules of gas.

The ideal gas law

The behaviour of ideal gases is represented by the **ideal gas equation**:

$$PV = nRT$$

where P is the pressure, measured in pascals, Pa; V is the volume, measured in metre cubed, m^3; T is the temperature on the Kelvin scale, measured in kelvins, K (notice that the degrees sign, °, is *not* put next to the K of a Kelvin temperature); R is the gas constant, $8.314\,J\,K^{-1}\,mol^{-1}$; and n is the number of moles of gas.

If pairs of measurements of V and T taken around room temperature are plotted and the lines extended back, they meet at (almost) $-273\,°C$. At this temperature, the volume of the gases appears to reduce to zero. Clearly, this is impossible for real gases, but none the less the graphs show that the temperature is of great importance. We can use the $-273\,°C$ point on the graph to define the zero of a new scale of temperature. This is the **absolute scale** or **Kelvin scale**. We can convert between degrees Celsius and kelvins by adding 273; e.g. $100\,°C = (100 + 273)\,K = 373\,K$. Similarly, we convert kelvins to degrees Celsius by subtracting 273; e.g. $127\,K = (127 - 273)\,°C = -146\,°C$.

When you use the equation, do be careful about the units. All the units given above are consistent; but sometimes you may have to use data that are given in other units. Especially, chemists often prefer to work in litres (more properly stated as dm^3) or in cm^3. Here is a way to change between these units:

$$1\,m^3 = 1 \times 10^3\,dm^3 = 1 \times 10^6\,cm^3$$

Also, pressure is often quoted in kilopascals, kPa, where $1\,kPa = 10^3\,Pa$. An old unit of pressure is the atmosphere, where 1 atmosphere is approximately $100\,kPa$. You may find that the volumes of gases are often quoted in litres or, more systematically, in dm^3. The relationship between the units of volume is as follows:

$$1\,litre = 1\,dm^3 = 1000\,cm^3 = 10^{-3}\,m^3$$

Worked example

What is the volume, given in dm^3, of 1 mol of an ideal gas at 20 °C and 100 kPa? (This combination of temperature and pressure is often called 'room temperature and pressure'.)

We have to convert the pressure to pascals and the temperature to kelvins: so we have $P = 100 \times 10^3\,Pa$, $T = (20 + 273)\,K = 293\,K$, $R = 8.314\,J\,K^{-1}\,mol^{-1}$, and $n = 1\,mol$. Putting these values into the ideal gas equation gives

$$100 \times 10^3\,Pa \times V = 1\,mol \times 8.314\,J\,K\,mol^{-1} \times 293\,K$$
$$V = \frac{1\,mol \times 8.314\,J\,K\,mol^{-1} \times 293\,K}{100 \times 10^3\,Pa}$$
$$V = 0.024\,m^3$$

Converting this to dm^3 gives $V = 24.4\,dm^3$. We usually make the approximation that 1 mol of gas occupies $24\,dm^3$ at room temperature and pressure.

SAQ 1.7

If a balloon contained $1\,dm^3$ of helium at 20°C and $100\,kPa$ pressure, how many moles of helium would be present?

SAQ 1.8

A weather balloon (*figure 1.22*) may have an 'envelope' of material that may contain a total volume of, say, $1000\,dm^3$ when it is fully expanded. However, the volume of helium put in the balloon when it is released into the atmosphere is only a fraction of this volume. Why is the balloon not fully inflated before it is released?

● **Figure 1.22** A weather balloon being released.

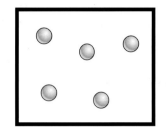

● **Figure 1.23** A *very* exaggerated impression of molecules taking up space – see text.

The behaviour of real gases

One of the obvious ways that real gases differ from ideal gases is that they liquefy when the temperature is low enough and the pressure is high enough. Lowering the temperature of real gases allows the intermolecular forces to over-come the motion of the molecules. Squeezing the molecules together has a similar effect: bringing molecules closer together allows the intermolecular forces to be more effective (just as bringing the north and south poles of magnets close together increases the effects of their attractive forces).

Only ideal gases would strictly obey the ideal gas equation. All real gases show deviations from ideal behaviour for two reasons:

1 The molecules in real gases take up space.
2 Real gases have intermolecular forces between the molecules.

We shall consider each of these factors in more detail now.

Real molecules occupy space

In an ideal gas, it is assumed that the molecules do not occupy space (see *box 1A*), so the volume in which they exist is (literally) the volume of the container. However, for real gases, each molecule takes up a very small volume (of the order of $10^{-30}\,m^3$), which is then not available for another molecule to move in. There are so many molecules that the total volume they occupy cannot be ignored. *Figure 1.23* illustrates this idea.

As a very simple analogy, consider a box with a volume of $1000\,cm^3$, in which there are five balls, with a volume of $20\,cm^3$ each. Between them they take up $100\,cm^3$, which is 10% of the total volume. Thus the volume open to them is at least 10% less than the volume of the container. The situation for molecules is just the same, although of a different scale. (Actually, calculating the real volume for the balls to move in is more complicated than we have assumed, but you don't have to know the details of why this is so.)

SAQ 1.9

Assume that the effective volume of an oxygen molecule is $64 \times 10^{-30}\,m^3$.

a Estimate the volume occupied by 1 mol of oxygen molecules. Avagadro's number $= 6.02 \times 10^{23}\,mol^{-1}$

b What percentage of the volume of 1 mol of oxygen gas is this at room temperature and pressure?

The influence of intermolecular forces

Intermolecular forces bring molecules together. These forces are always present in gases, even though a gas is only a gas because the intermolecular forces are not strong enough to prevent the molecules bouncing apart when they collide. Think about what happens if a molecule is moving out of the main body of a gas towards the walls of the container (see *figure 1.24* overleaf). The vast majority of molecules will be attracting it from behind, or from its sides. This tends to slow the molecule and prevent it colliding with the walls of the container with as much force as it would do if there were no intermolecular forces. In other words, the pressure exerted by a real gas is *less* than it would be if the gas were ideal.

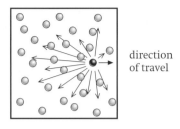

direction of travel

● **Figure 1.24** A molecule moving out of the main volume of the gas feels an overall force attracting it inwards.

Summary table

	Molecules in an ideal gas	Molecules in a real gas	Effect in real gases
Occupation of space by molecules	None	Occupy space	Reduces volume from ideal value
Intermolecular forces	None	Present, and can be strong	Reduces pressure from ideal value

● **Table 1.3** Summary of differences between real and ideal gases.

Real gases can approach ideal behaviour

Remember that two of the conditions for ideal behaviour were that the molecules were of negligible size and that there were no intermolecular forces. We can sometimes come close to these conditions for real gases if:

1 we use gases that have very small intermolecular forces between the molecules;
2 we use gases at very low pressures.

Gases like hydrogen and helium fulfil the first condition; and by using very low pressures, the molecules of a gas spend a great deal of their time far apart from each other. This results in the intermolecular forces not having a chance to work effectively. It also means that because there are very few molecules in a given space at low pressures, the volume that the molecules do occupy is a very small proportion of the total; i.e. their own volume does become nearly negligible.

SAQ 1.10

In your own words, explain why, at low pressures, real gases begin to behave more like ideal gases.

Measuring the relative molecular mass of a volatile liquid

We shall now use the ideal gas equation to calculate the relative molecular mass of a volatile liquid. This may, at first sight, seem rather an odd statement given that the ideal gas equation plainly applies to gases and not to liquids. However, the key to the puzzle is that the method relies on turning the liquid into a gas. Before you go on, you should remind yourself about the mole as a measure of the quantity of matter in chemistry (see *Chemistry 1*, page 19).

SAQ 1.11

What is the approximate volume of **a** 2 mol and **b** 0.25 mol of carbon dioxide at room temperature and pressure?

The method

There are several ways of performing this experiment. The method we shall choose is to use the apparatus shown in *figure 1.25*.

The outline of the method is as follows:

1 Take a known mass of the volatile liquid.
2 Introduce the liquid into a gas syringe in an oven.
3 Turn the liquid to vapour and measure its volume.

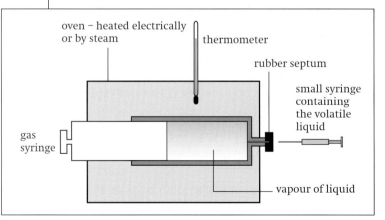

oven – heated electrically or by steam

thermometer

rubber septum

small syringe containing the volatile liquid

gas syringe

vapour of liquid

● **Figure 1.25** One method of measuring the volume of a volatile liquid using a gas syringe and an oven.

Knowing the gas volume and its temperature, we can use the ideal gas equation to work out how many moles of gas are present. Then, because we know the mass of this number of moles, we can work out the relative molecular mass of the gas, and hence of the liquid.

The nozzle of the gas syringe is covered with a rubber cap (a septum), and the gas syringe is put in the oven or steam jacket. Once the reading on the gas syringe shows no further change, the initial reading on the gas syringe is taken, and a sample of the liquid is taken up into a small syringe. Here, we shall assume that we are using ethoxyethane (ether) as the liquid. The small syringe is weighed and the ethoxyethane injected into the gas syringe. Then the small syringe is immediately reweighed. Once the ethoxyethane is in the gas syringe, the liquid quickly vaporises and the plunger is driven outwards. Eventually equilibrium is achieved and there is no further change in the volume recorded on the gas syringe. Provided the temperature of the steam jacket and the atmospheric pressure are known we can calculate the relative molecular mass.

Some sample results

Here are some sample readings:

Mass of small syringe and ethoxyethane
before injection into gas syringe = 20.476 g
after injection into gas syringe = 20.252 g
Initial reading on gas syringe = 1.4 cm^3
Final reading on gas syringe = 96.8 cm^3
Temperature of steam jacket (oven) = 99.6 °C
= 372.6 K
Atmospheric pressure = 100 kPa

From these results we have

Mass of ethoxyethane used = 0.224 g
Volume of vapour = 95.4 cm^3
= 95.4 × 10^{-6} m^3

We can use the ideal gas equation to work out the number of moles, n, of ethoxyethane that this volume represents. We have

$$PV = nRT$$

or

$$n = \frac{PV}{RT}$$

$$n = \frac{100 \times 10^3 \, Pa \times 95.4 \times 10^{-6} \, m^3}{8.314 \, J \, K^{-1} \, mol^{-1} \times 372.6 \, K}$$
$$= 0.003 \, mol$$

$$\text{Relative molecular mass} = \frac{0.224 \, g}{0.003 \, mol}$$
$$= 74.7 \, g \, mol^{-1}$$

Experimental error

The formula of ethoxyethane is $(C_2H_5)_2O$, so its true relative molecular mass is 74 g mol^{-1}. It is quite common for results in this experiment to over-estimate relative molecular masses. The most important reason for this is that, before the liquid can be injected into the gas syringe, some if it evaporates from the needle of the small syringe. This means that we over-estimate the mass of liquid that turns into gas in the gas syringe. For example, in our calculation above, the actual mass of liquid injected into the gas syringe may have been only 0.223 g. Then the relative molecular mass would have been calculated as 0.223 g/0.003 mol = 74.33 g mol^{-1}. (If the true mass injected were 0.222 g, the result would have been exactly 74 g mol^{-1}, the true relative molecular mass.)

SAQ 1.12
The gas syringe experiment only works with liquids that are highly volatile, i.e. those which evaporate easily.
a   Explain why the mass of liquid injected into the gas syringe is often *less* than that given by the weighings.
b   How, and why, does this affect the calculation?

SAQ 1.13
The volatile liquid propanone was used in an experiment to measure its relative molecular mass, like the one we have discussed above. The following data were collected:

Mass of syringe and propanone
before injection into gas syringe = 20.374 g
Mass of syringe and propanone
after injection into gas syringe = 20.193 g
Initial reading on gas syringe = 1.6 cm^3
Final reading on gas syringe = 97.1 cm^3
Temperature of steam jacket (oven) = 99.3 °C
Atmospheric pressure = 100.2 kPa

Calculate the relative molecular mass of propanone.

SUMMARY

◆ The three states of matter are solid, liquid and gas. The state a substance exists in depends on the kinetic energy of the particles and the strength of the inter-molecular forces between its particles.

◆ The particles in a solid have orderly arrangements; liquids have short-range order but long-range disorder; gases have completely disorderly arrangements of their particles.

◆ The space between gas particles is very much greater than the spaces between the particles in a solid or liquid. The spacing of particles in a liquid and solid is about the same.

◆ As the kinetic energy of particles increases, the temperature increases, intermolecular forces are overcome and solids tend to melt, and liquids turn to gas.

◆ Substances that have hydrogen bonds between their molecules often have unusually high melting and boiling points, e.g. H_2O, HF.

◆ Liquids have a characteristic vapour pressure at a given temperature and pressure. In a closed system, an equilibrium is set up such that the rate at which molecules leave the liquid equals the rate at which gaseous molecules return to the liquid.

◆ A liquid boils when its vapour pressure equals the atmospheric pressure.

◆ The key assumptions about ideal gases are:
  – The molecules have mass, but negligible size.
  – There are no intermolecular forces.

◆ The kinetic theory of gases claims that:
  – Gases consist of molecules in a constant state of random motion.
  – The pressure of a gas is due to the collisions of the molecules with the walls of the container.
  – The molecules travel in straight lines until they collide with one another, or with the walls of the container.
  – In these collisions the total kinetic energy of the molecules does not change.

◆ Ideal gases obey the ideal gas equation, $PV = nRT$.

◆ Real gases show deviations from ideal behaviour because:
  – the particles in a real gas occupy space;
  – real gases have intermolecular forces between their particles.

◆ Real gases approach ideal behaviour at (i) high temperature and (ii) low pressure.

◆ At low temperature and/or high pressure the intermolecular forces in real gases have a large effect and the behaviour of the gases are far from ideal.

◆ The relative molecular mass of a volatile liquid can be measured by: (i) weighing a sample; (ii) injecting the sample into a gas syringe held at a temperature greater than the liquid's boiling point; (iii) allowing equilibrium to be reached; (iv) measuring the temperature and volume of the vapour; and (v) using the ideal gas equation to calculate the number of moles of vapour present.

Questions

1 *Table 1.2* (page 5) and *figure 1.11* (page 6) provide information that you will need in order to answer this set of questions.

  a Why does carbon (as diamond) have such a high melting point?

  b What might be the reason for ammonia, NH_3, having an anomalous boiling point compared to other hydrides of Group V? [*Hint*: What is special about the structure of an ammonia molecule?]

  c What is the main type of bonding that holds the alkanes together in their solid or liquid states?

  d What is the main type of bonding that holds the alcohols together in their solid or liquid states?

  e How do the boiling points of the alkanes methane to butane compare with those of the corresponding alcohols methanol to butan-1-ol?

2 Use the data in *table 1.2* to sketch a diagram showing how the boiling points of the Group VII hydrides (HF, HCl, HBr and HI) vary. Explain the trend that you observe.

3 When water (or any liquid) boils, you can see bubbles appear in the liquid. What are the bubbles in boiling water?

4 Check back: What is the connection between vapour pressure, atmospheric pressure and the boiling point of a liquid? Now explain why it takes longer to cook vegetables in water at high altitudes (e.g. on the side of a high mountain) than at sea level.

5 Here is a question that will make you think about the repercussions of the idea that the particles in a gas are in a constant random motion. It will also bring home to you the relevance of the small scale of atoms and molecules compared to our everyday experience.

  The diagram represents a container filled with nitrogen gas. The container is connected to a vacuum pump by a small

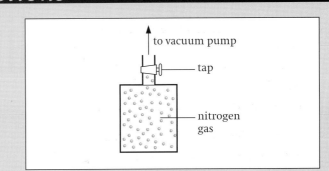

tube fitted with a tap. Please remember that the diagram is not to scale!

  a What, if anything, is in the space between the nitrogen molecules?

  b Suppose the tube connecting the container to the vacuum pump has a diameter of 1 cm. The diameter of a nitrogen molecule is approximately 4×10^{-10} m. How many nitrogen molecules could fit across the diameter of the tube?

  c Would a nitrogen molecule find it hard to find its way down the tube?

  d Using a rough value, assume you are about 1 m wide. If the tube were of the same scale to you as it is to a nitrogen molecule, how wide would it be? How does this distance compare to, say, the diameter of the Earth (about 3×10^6 m)?

  e Now imagine that the tap to the vacuum pump is opened very briefly so that some, but not all, of the nitrogen molecules escape. Draw a diagram like the one above to show what you think the arrangement of the molecules would be at the very instant the tap was closed.

  f Briefly explain why some of the gas would go into the vacuum pump when the tap was opened.

6 Trichloromethane (chloroform) has a boiling point of about 62 °C. On the face of it, this liquid should be a suitable candidate for using in the gas syringe experiment. Why might you expect its measured relative molecular mass not to be accurate? [*Hint*: Think about intermolecular forces.]

CHAPTER 2

Phase equilibria

By the end of this chapter you should be able to:

1 understand that *phase diagrams* are graphical plots of experimentally determined results;

2 interpret phase diagrams as *curves* describing the conditions of equilibrium between phases and as *regions* representing single phases;

3 predict how phases may alter with changes in temperature or pressure;

4 sketch the shape of the *phase diagram for water* and explain the anomalous behaviour of water;

5 understand and use the term *eutectic*;

6 interpret *phase diagrams for two-component systems* and predict how compositions and phases vary with changes in temperature;

7 sketch the shape of the phase diagram for *mixtures of tin and lead*;

8 state, and explain in simple terms, how the hardness and melting points of common *alloys* differ from those of pure metals;

9 sketch the shape of the *solubility curve* of a salt, such as NaCl in water;

10 sketch the shape of the phase diagram for a two-component system, such as NaCl and water.

What is a phase?

A short way of describing a **phase** is to say that:

> A phase has the same physical and chemical composition in all its parts.

A phase can be a solid, a liquid, or a gas (*figure 2.1*); it can also be a solution. The important thing is that every part of the solid, liquid, gas or solution must be the same as every other part. In short, it must be **homogeneous**. If you were to mix some coal and salt, you would have a mixture of two solids. It is most unlikely that the mixture would be exactly the same in every part. This mixture consists of two solid phases. However, if you were to melt a combination of silver and gold, thoroughly mix the resulting liquid, and then allow the liquid to solidify, you would find that the solid was homogeneous. Here there would be two elements but only one phase. The solid made is known as a solid solution.

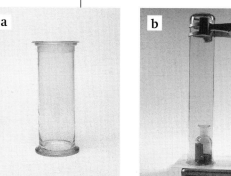

● **Figure 2.1** Each of the halogens **a** chlorine $Cl_2(g)$, **b** bromine $Br_2(l)$ and **c** iodine $I_2(s)$ exists in a different phase at room temperature and pressure, although bromine and iodine are volatile and easily vaporise.

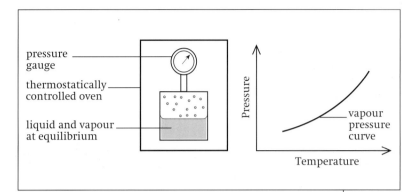

● **Figure 2.2** Outline of a method for an experiment to determine the vapour pressure curve of a liquid.

To begin with we shall ignore mixtures, whether they be solid solutions or not, and concentrate on the equilibria between the three phases of a pure substance: solid, liquid and gas. You do not need to know the details of how these equilibria are studied; but in outline the equilibrium between a liquid and its vapour could be investigated by using an apparatus like that shown in *figure 2.2*. The idea is to put the liquid under test in a cylinder, which is itself inside an oven whose temperature can be carefully controlled. We could change the temperature, leave the liquid and vapour to come to equilibrium, and then measure the pressure that the vapour exerts in the cylinder. (Note that the pressure exerted by the vapour is a property of the liquid in question, and it is *not* the same as the atmospheric pressure outside the apparatus.) By repeating the experiment at different temperatures, we would be able to plot the pairs of values on a graph. The resulting line is known as a **vapour pressure curve**. Typically it has the shape shown in *figure 2.2*.

By the way, you may have noticed that we usually use the word 'vapour' to describe the molecules of a liquid when they are in the gaseous state. Similarly, we shall often talk about the vapour phase (rather than the gaseous phase).

How to interpret a phase diagram

A **phase diagram** for a substance shows the equilibrium (i) between liquid and vapour, (ii) between solid and liquid and (iii) between solid and vapour. A typical example is shown in *figure 2.3*, where you will find the phase diagram for

carbon dioxide – the diagram is not drawn to scale.

The phase diagram is made up of three lines, which are known as the **vapour pressure curve**, the **melting point curve** and the **sublimation curve**.

- *Vapour pressure curve CT.* The line CT shows what happens to the boiling point of carbon dioxide as the pressure changes. It is a gentle curve. On one side of the line there is the label 'liquid CO_2', and on the other 'gaseous CO_2'. In this case the vapour pressure curve (also called boiling point curve) CT represents a series of points at which liquid and gaseous CO_2 can be in equilibrium.

- *Melting point curve BT.* The line BT shows what happens to the melting point of carbon dioxide as the pressure changes. It is very nearly a straight line. On one side of the line there is the label 'solid CO_2', and on the other 'liquid CO_2'. This tells us what is happening at each pair of values of the pressure and temperature. In fact the melting point curve BT represents a series of points at which solid and liquid CO_2 can be in equilibrium.

- *Sublimation curve AT.* The line AT tells us about the equilibrium that can exist between solid CO_2 and gaseous CO_2. The change directly from solid to gas is known as 'sublimation'. Thus, the line AT shows the values of pressure and temperature when solid CO_2 will sublime.

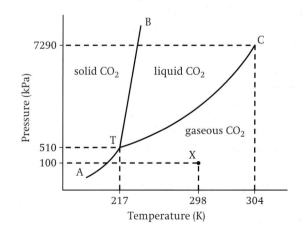

● **Figure 2.3** The phase diagram for carbon dioxide, used as a typical example. (Note that the diagram is *not* to scale.)

The phase diagram also has two points that you will need to recognise: the **triple point** and the **critical point**.

■ *Triple point T.* You can see that the three lines CT, BT and AT meet, at the point T. Here, solid, liquid and gaseous CO_2 can be present together; but there is only one combination of pressure and temperature at which this can happen. For fairly obvious reasons, the point T is called the *triple point*. For carbon dioxide, the triple point comes at a pressure of 510 kPa, and temperature 217 K. This is the *only* set of conditions at which all three phases (solid, liquid and gas) can be in equilibrium.

■ *Critical point C.* Finally, this point gives the temperature above which it is impossible to liquefy a gas, and where separate phases (liquid and gas) become one indistinguishable phase.

These various parts of a typical phase diagram are summarised in *table 2.1*.

For a phase diagram it is important that you realise the following:

1 The lines represent a series of points at which the phases involved can be *at equilibrium*.
2 The lines are plotted from data obtained from experiment.

At points that are not on any of the lines, only one phase can be present (under equilibrium conditions). Look at *figure 2.3* in more detail for a moment. You can see that at 298 K and 100 kPa pressure (roughly room temperature and pressure) the point X corresponding to this pair of conditions does not lie on any of the lines. In fact, it lies below the vapour pressure curve, which indicates that carbon dioxide will be a gas at

● **Figure 2.4** Carbon dioxide is used to decaffeinate coffee. It removes the caffeine without significantly damaging the flavour.

room temperature and pressure. This confirms what you should already know about the gas. At other points on the phase diagram, carbon dioxide will behave differently. Carbon dioxide is used in the decaffeination of coffee (*figure 2.4*).

The phase diagram also shows us that melting and boiling points change with pressure. This is the reason why, for example, it was stated in *table 1.2* that the values there were measured at standard atmospheric pressure. (Strictly, whenever melting or boiling points are stated, the pressure should also be mentioned; but usually we assume that standard atmospheric pressure is meant.)

	Name	**Comment**
Lines		
CT	Vapour pressure curve	Liquid and vapour in equilibrium – the process of evaporation
BT	Melting point curve	Solid and liquid in equilibrium – the process of melting (melting point 'curves' are usually very nearly straight lines)
AT	Sublimation curve	Solid and vapour in equilibrium – the process of sublimation
Points		
T	Triple point	Only set of conditions at which all three phases can be in equilibrium
C	Critical point	Temperature above which it is impossible to liquefy a gas, and where separate phases become indistinguishable

● **Table 2.1** Common parts of phase diagrams for many substances (*see figure 2.3*).

SAQ 2.1

'Dry ice' is solid carbon dioxide. It is used in the entertainment industry to give off clouds of steamy-looking vapour on stage (*figure 2.5*).

a Sketch a copy of the phase diagram of carbon dioxide and show on it the temperature at which dry ice would be in equilibrium with the vapour phase, i.e. sublime, at 100 kPa pressure.

b Use the diagram to explain why no liquid carbon dioxide is seen creeping over the stage.

c Does this use of dry ice take place at equilibrium?

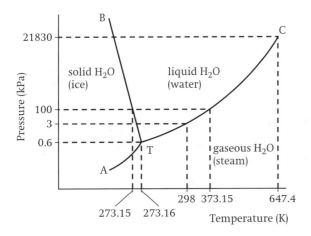

● **Figure 2.5** Clouds of dry ice create an unusual effect at a pop concert.

The phase diagram of water

The phase diagram of water is shown in *figures 2.6* and *2.7*. (Please note that the diagrams are *not* drawn to scale, and the figures on the pressure axes have been rounded off. You will need to take account of this if you look at other books, or

● **Figure 2.6** The phase diagram for water, showing the regions in which the three phases occur. (Note that the diagram is not drawn to scale.)

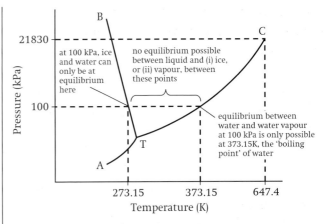

● **Figure 2.7** The phase diagram for water, showing the equilibria that exist at 100 kPa. (Note that the diagram is not drawn to scale.)

tables of data, and find that the values given are different.) Two diagrams are shown so that you can see more clearly the different pieces of information. In the remainder of this chapter you may have to look at just one or both figures as you read the text or answer the questions.

The first thing to notice is that the general appearance of the diagram is similar to that for carbon dioxide: there are the three major lines, together with the critical point and triple point (although the ranges of temperatures and pressures are quite different). However, there is one key difference that is unusual in phase diagrams. The melting point curve BT (i.e. the ice/water equilibrium) slopes up to the left rather than up to the right. The reason for this is complicated, but concerns the fact that the solid phase of water (ice) is *less* dense than the liquid phase. For most substances (like carbon dioxide), the solid phase is *more* dense than the liquid. If pressure increases on such a substance, it favours the production of the solid phase; but with water the reverse is true, and an increase of pressure favours the melting of ice. The way that this shows up on phase diagrams is that the slopes of the melting point curves go in opposite directions.

You will also see that at 100 kPa pressure the point on the vapour pressure curve CT comes at a temperature of 373.15 K, and not 373 K. We use 373 K as the boiling point of water; but this is only approximately true – the value 373.15 K is the accurate value for the normal boiling point of water. Likewise, at 100 kPa pressure the equilibrium temperature on the melting point curve BT is 273.15 K, and not 273 K. (Again, the latter value is only an approximation.)

SAQ 2.2

Look at *figures 2.6* and *2.7*.
a What are the pressure and temperature at the triple point of water?
b Describe what is happening to water that has a vapour pressure of 3 kPa and a temperature of 298 K.
c Above what temperature will steam never condense to liquid water?
d At normal atmospheric pressure, can ice be made to sublime (i.e. turn directly into a vapour without going through a liquid stage)? Briefly explain your answer.

Equilibrium between a solid and a liquid

What happens when a liquid freezes?

The particles in a liquid are held together by inter-molecular forces. It is the strength of these forces that prevents the liquid from changing completely into a gas. You may remember that the particles have a spread of energies: some have much less energy than the average, and some have a lot more. However, on average, the particles in a liquid have sufficient energy to keep them jiggling about and prevent the intermolecular forces from making them stick together permanently. When we cool a liquid, the average energy of the particles goes down, and then the intermolecular forces can win the battle; the particles are attracted strongly together, and crystals appear.

The temperature at which a solid turns into a liquid is its **melting point**. More accurately we should say that:

> The melting point is the temperature at which solid and liquid can exist in equilibrium with each other at 100 kPa pressure.

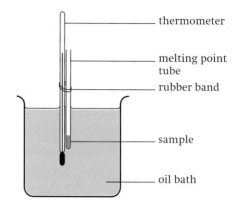

● **Figure 2.8** A simple melting point apparatus. If the sample is pure, it should have a sharp melting point.

Above the melting point, the solid will change completely into liquid. Below the melting point, the liquid will change completely into solid. A melting point can be determined either by increasing the temperature until a solid melts, or by cooling a liquid until it begins to crystallise. The two temperatures should be the same value, because there is only one set of conditions at which the solid can be in equilibrium with its liquid.

Both methods of determining melting point have their uses. For example, determining the melting point by heating is used in chemistry as a way of identifying a compound. The method relies on the fact that every pure substance has its own characteristic melting point. A simple apparatus used to determine a melting point (usually of an organic compound) by heating is shown in *figure 2.8*. The method using cooling is covered in the next subsection.

Cooling curve for a pure substance

The most accurate way of finding the melting point of a solid is by taking the liquid and allowing it to cool. It is interesting to plot a graph of temperature against time in such an experiment. The resulting graph is known as a **cooling curve**. *Figure 2.9* illustrates two simple ways of measuring cooling curves, and *figure 2.10* illustrates a typical cooling curve obtained for the organic compound naphthalene.

The naphthalene is heated to some way above its melting point, making sure all the solid has liquefied. Then the tube is allowed to cool slowly

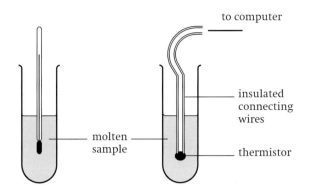

● **Figure 2.9** A cooling curve can be measured directly with a mercury-in-glass thermometer, or by using a thermistor (or thermocouple) connected to a computer interface. Using a computer, the measurement of temperature can be automated at pre-defined time intervals. (The thermistor has to be calibrated before it is used.)

and the temperature taken at a fixed time interval (e.g. every two minutes). The pattern of observations in *figure 2.10* is typical. The general trend for the temperature is as follows: first it decreases steadily, then it rises briefly before remaining constant, and finally it decreases again until room temperature is reached. The explanation for this series of events is as follows.

Initially, the whole sample is liquid, and as the sample loses heat to the surroundings the average kinetic energy of the molecules falls. But until the kinetic energy drops to a low enough level, the molecules continue to bounce off one another. Eventually, the molecules lose sufficient energy and the intermolecular forces take over: the molecules begin to stick together and crystals appear.

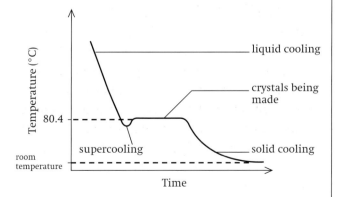

● **Figure 2.10** A cooling curve for naphthalene. The melting point of naphthalene is 80.4 °C at 100 kPa pressure.

That is, the intermolecular forces are making bonds between the molecules.

Making bonds is an **exothermic** process, and it is the heat given out when crystals are made that stops the temperature falling. The heat released also has the effect of raising the temperature of the liquid. This prevents more crystals appearing until some of the heat is dissipated into the surroundings; then more crystals appear, giving out more heat, which stops the temperature falling – and so on. Eventually, all the liquid crystallises, and the crystals cool to room temperature.

Often there is a dip in the cooling curve just before crystals appear. This dip in temperature is known as **supercooling**. It can happen that the particles in the liquid fail to join up to make crystals. If this happens, we say that the liquid has entered a **metastable state**. A metastable state is easily disturbed, for example by the liquid being shaken, or a speck of dust entering it. When the first few crystals are made, the energy released causes the temperature to rise rapidly to the normal melting point.

SAQ 2.3
In *figure 2.10* the legend says that the melting point of naphthalene is 80.4 °C *at 100 kPa pressure*.
a Why should melting points always be stated at a given pressure?
b What phases should be in equilibrium when the cooling curve becomes horizontal?
c Why is it important that the sample is allowed to cool slowly?

Cooling curves for mixtures
You may know that the freezing point of a liquid is depressed if it contains another substance dissolved in it. For example, salt water will freeze below 0 °C at atmospheric pressure. Similar depressions occur with other mixtures. One mixture that is very widely used in the electronics industry is solder (*figure 2.11* overleaf). Solder is a mixture of tin and lead. (However, if you buy a reel of solder, it will almost certainly contain a third substance: the flux. The flux helps to stop the two metals from oxidising when they get hot.) Pure lead melts at 328 °C, and pure tin melts at 232 °C.

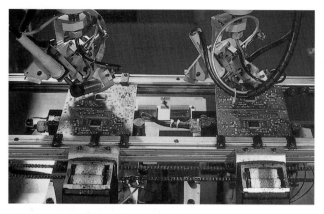

● **Figure 2.11** These robots are using solder to construct complex circuit boards.

However, a mixture of the two melts at a lower temperature than either of them individually. Solder that contains almost twice as much tin as lead has a cooling curve like that in *figure 2.12a*. This cooling curve has the same shape as we find for a pure substance. When the liquid crystallises, the solid made has exactly the same composition as the original mixture. The mixture of approximately 64% tin and 36% lead by mass is called the **eutectic** mixture.

If you were to take a eutectic mixture and melt it, you would find that it had a sharp melting point; i.e. the whole mixture would begin to melt at the same temperature. All other mixtures melt over a fairly wide range of temperatures; i.e their melting points are not sharp. One way of spotting the eutectic mixture on a phase diagram is that

the eutectic mixture has the lowest melting point of all the possible mixtures of the metals.

Mixtures that do not have the same composition as the eutectic have a cooling curve like that in *figure 2.12b*. The big difference is that the curve has a bend in it before the flat portion is reached. If we take a mixture containing 25% tin and 75% lead, the bend occurs at about 270 °C. At this temperature, crystals begin to be made. The crystals are pure lead. As the crystals are made, some heat is given out, and this makes the mixture cool more slowly. Because the solution loses lead, the liquid remaining becomes richer in tin. Eventually, the liquid reaches the eutectic composition (64% tin), at which time the remaining liquid crystallises to give a solid with the eutectic composition. This gives the usual flat part on the cooling curve. The period during which the temperature stays constant while the eutectic crystallises is known as the **eutectic halt**.

The phase diagram for a mixture of tin and lead

Imagine making up a series of mixtures of tin and lead by accurately weighing out samples of the two metals. Then you could melt each mixture one at a time (making sure that the liquids were well mixed), and allow them to cool. For every

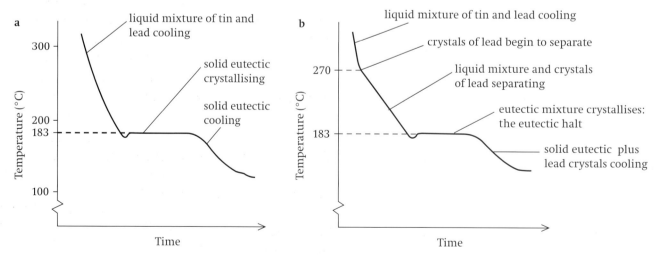

● **Figure 2.12**
a Cooling curve for a eutectic mixture of (approximately) 64% tin and 36% lead (by mass). The mixture behaves like a pure substance.
b Cooling curve for a mixture of 25% tin and 75% lead (by mass). At 270 °C, lead crystals appear. More lead crystallises until at 183 °C the eutectic mixture separates.

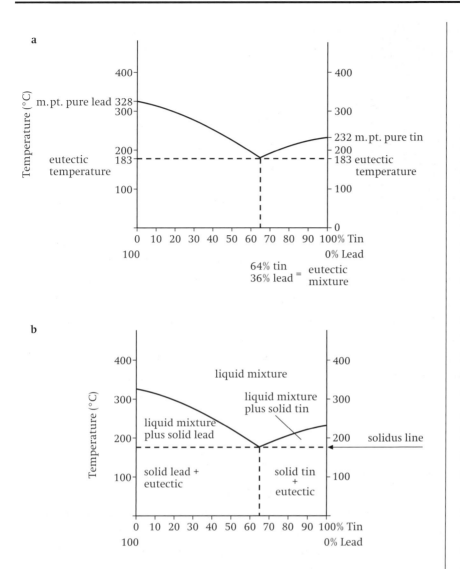

● **Figure 2.13**
a Phase diagram (or melting point–composition diagram) for a mixture of tin and lead.
b Composition of the various regions on the diagram. (Note that this is a simplified version that ignores many details of the complete diagram, and the pressure is assumed to be 100 kPa.)

mixture, you would note the temperature at which some solid starts to separate. Then, if you were to plot these temperatures against the proportions of the two metals in the mixtures, you would find a graph that looks like *figure 2.13a*. This figure shows how the melting points of mixtures of tin and lead change with the composition of the mixtures. This figure is the tin–lead phase diagram. It can also be called the melting point–composition diagram for mixtures of tin and lead.

Incidentally, you may wonder why it is that, if we do the experiment by cooling the liquid mixtures, the diagram is called a 'melting point' diagram. If we were to melt the mixtures, we should be able to discover the temperature at which it just begins to melt. This would be the same temperature as we measure in the cooling method. (The same solid–liquid equilibrium is involved.) However, in practice, it is

far easier to use the cooling method, because then we do not have the problem of trying to heat all parts of a solid mixture to the same temperature.

Sometimes the phase diagram has labels added to it. For example, *figure 2.13b* shows that, below the line to the left-hand side of the eutectic, there will be solid lead in contact with liquid. In the similar region to the right of the eutectic, there will be solid tin in contact with liquid. Below the eutectic temperature, 183 °C, only solid is present. This gives rise to the name **solidus** for the (imaginary) line that stretches across the diagram at the eutectic temperature. To the left of the eutectic the solid will consist of lead and eutectic, and to the right of the eutectic the solid will contain tin and eutectic.

Eutectics are not chemical compounds. If a eutectic is examined under a microscope, separate small crystals of the components can be seen. Also, the composition of a eutectic rarely conforms to that expected for a compound. For example, the tin–lead eutectic has a 'formula' that approximately corresponds to $Sn_{2.8}Pb_{2.5}$. A summary of the properties of eutectics is given in *box 2A*.

Box 2A Properties of eutectics
A eutectic has:
■ a sharp melting point like a pure substance;
■ the lowest melting point of all the mixtures;
■ a cooling curve like a pure substance;
■ no simple formula, and is not a compound.

SAQ 2.4

Look at the diagram in *figure 2.14* for a mixture of X and Y.

a Sketch the cooling curves that you would expect to obtain if you were to use mixtures of composition (i) A, (ii) B and (iii) C at the temperatures shown by the dotted lines.

b Say what would be present in the five regions labelled (i) P, (ii) Q, (iii) R, (iv) S and (v) T. (Regions Q, R, S and T are each shaded differently. In this part, ignore the dotted lines drawn from A and 250 °C, and from C and 175 °C.)

c Carefully explain what would happen when a mixture that begins life at a temperature and composition given by the point M on the diagram is cooled to room temperature.

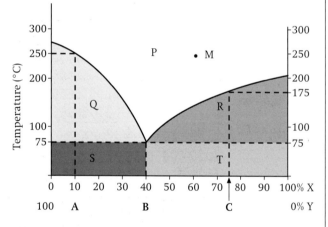

● **Figure 2.14** Melting point–composition diagram for a mixture of X and Y.

Name	Composition	Use
Solder	Tin and lead of varying proportions	In plumbing to seal joints where metal pipes meet. In the electronics industry to make good electrical, and physical, connections between components
Steel	Iron with small amounts of C and Mn	Car bodies, bridges, etc., where strength but greater ductility and malleability than iron is needed
Stainless steel	Iron with up to 35% Cr	Steel with great resistance to corrosion, e.g. knives, sinks, industrial pipes, jet engines
Coinage metal	Cu 75%, Ni 25% Cu 97%, Sn 0.5%, Zn 2.5%	'Silver' coins 'Copper' coins
Brass	Various proportions of copper and zinc, e.g. Cu 70%, Zn 30%	Door knobs, ornaments, bullet cases
Duralumin	Aluminium with up to 5% Cu, less than 1% Mn, Mg and Si	In aircraft, owing to combination of strength with lightness
Monel	About 66% Ni, 33% Cu with some Fe, Mn, Si and C	Equipment that must be resistant to corrosion, e.g. in steam turbines
Nichrome	Ni 60%, Fe 20%, Cr 20%	Wires for electrical equipment

● **Table 2.2** Examples of alloys.

The properties of alloys vary with the proportions of their constituents. For example, as with solder (an alloy of tin and lead), the melting point of an alloy is generally below that of the pure metals. However, it is not only the melting point that can change; often the hardness, brittleness, appearance and resistance to corrosion change as well. It is one of the tasks of metallurgists to study the properties of alloys and to choose a particular alloy for a particular purpose. You can find a list of common alloys and their uses in *table 2.2*.

One of the most common alloys that we use is the stuff we know as steel. In fact, there are very many different types of steel, but they are all composed mainly of iron, together with a small amount of carbon, and small quantities of other elements are added as well (especially Si, V, Cr, Mn, Mo, Co, Ni, P and S). Pure iron rusts very easily, and when it is cast into moulds, it is not shiny and is brittle. The addition of even a little carbon and/or another element to molten iron changes these properties markedly, depending on the quantity of the added elements. On cooling to a solid, the steel produced has a bright shiny surface (i.e. it is lustrous), is not brittle, can be rolled

Alloys

We can define an **alloy** as follows:

Alloys are mixtures containing a metal and at least one other element (metallic or non-metallic).

into thin sheets (i.e. it is malleable) or pulled into wires (i.e. ductile), and is more resistant to corrosion. Steel also retains much of the strength of iron, and this combination of properties makes steel ideal for products ranging from cutlery to car, ship and aeroplane bodies. Many of the most important alloys contain transition metals.

The explanation of why the addition of a different type of atom can change the physical properties of an element so greatly is complicated. However, one of the key reasons lies in the different sizes of the atoms involved. You can gain some insight into the reason if you look at *figure 2.15*, which illustrates the effect of the introduction of a larger atom into a lattice of metal atoms. Although the 'foreign' atom changes the lattice, this can stop the lattice from being disrupted by a sudden shock as easily as that of the pure metal. The imperfections in a lattice can also reduce the strength of the metallic bonding and make it easier for the atoms to move their positions, which leads to alloys having melting points lower than those of their parent metals. However, everything depends on the precise nature of the majority metal and the foreign atoms. For example, often the foreign atoms are smaller than those of the majority metal, and their concentration has a major influence on the properties of the alloy.

SAQ 2.5

By hand or using a computer graphics program, try drawing diagrams like those in *figure 2.15*, but with a metal lattice containing an impurity atom that is *smaller* than the metal atoms. Is the lattice disrupted?

The solubility of salts in water

The solubility of a solid in water is usually given as the number of grams of the solid that will dissolve in 100 g of water at a given temperature. *Table 2.3* shows typical values of solubilities at 25 °C. Ionic crystals often dissolve endothermically in water, and their solubilities usually, but not always, increase with temperature. However, the extent of the increase varies greatly, as shown in *figure 2.16* overleaf. Be careful to note that the way solubilities change with temperature does not tell us *how fast* a substance will dissolve. A substance may have a very high solubility in water, but it still might take a long time to dissolve completely. Also, notice that the change in solubility of sodium chloride with temperature is almost a horizontal line, but this is not typical.

To measure the solubility of a solid, there has to be undissolved solid present in the liquid. This means that an equilibrium can be set up between the particles of the solid and those dissolved in the liquid. *Figure 2.17* overleaf gives an exaggerated impression of this. When equilibrium is reached, the rate at which ions leave the solid is just

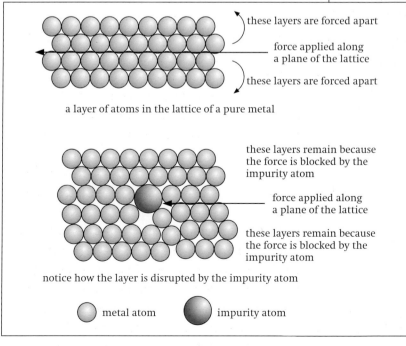

a layer of atoms in the lattice of a pure metal

these layers are forced apart

force applied along a plane of the lattice

these layers are forced apart

these layers remain because the force is blocked by the impurity atom

force applied along a plane of the lattice

these layers remain because the force is blocked by the impurity atom

notice how the layer is disrupted by the impurity atom

○ metal atom   ● impurity atom

● **Figure 2.15** A two-dimensional representation of how the introduction of a large impurity atom disrupts a lattice of metal atoms.

Substance	Solubility (g per 100 g of water)
NaCl	35.98
NaBr	94.57
NaI	184.25
$MgSO_4$	22.01
$CaSO_4$	0.63
$BaSO_4$	2.2×10^{-4}
$Ba(NO_3)_2$	10.22
$NaNO_3$	91.69

● **Table 2.3** Solubilities of salts in water at 25 °C.

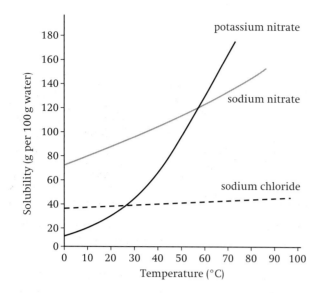

● **Figure 2.16** Solubility curves for three ionic substances in water.

balanced by the rate at which ions leave the liquid and rejoin the solid. At equilibrium, we say that the solution is **saturated**, i.e. it contains the maximum amount of solid dissolved that is possible at the given temperature.

There is a wide range of solubilities of salts, and it is not easy to draw up hard-and-fast rules that can be used to predict the values. However, major factors are the strength of the solid's lattice, and the strength of the attraction between the ions and water molecules. The stronger the lattice (i.e. the higher the lattice energy), the more likely it is that the substance will not dissolve easily; on the other hand, the more strongly attracted the ions are by water molecules, the more likely the solid is to dissolve.

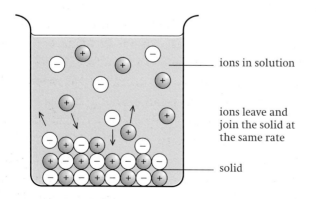

● **Figure 2.17** An exaggerated impression of the equilibrium between an ionic solid and its solution.

SAQ 2.6
Revise the work you have done on Le Chatelier's principle (*Chemistry 1*, page 181, and *Chemistry 2*, page 125), and then say why you might predict that solubilities increase with temperature for substances that dissolve endothermically in water.

The phase diagram for common salt in water

The phase diagram for mixtures of common salt (sodium chloride) and water (*figure 2.18*) is complicated by a number of factors. One of these is that, depending on the temperature and the concentration of the solution, sodium chloride can exist as a **hydrate** in the solution rather than just simple NaCl. The hydrate has the formula $NaCl.2H_2O$, but where the change to 'ordinary' NaCl occurs, the phase diagram becomes complicated. It is for this reason that only part of the complete diagram is shown in *figures 2.18* and *2.19*. Also, for the sake of simplicity, the regions have been labelled with the word 'salt' rather than including details of the hydrate. However, you can see that in most respects the diagram is similar to those we looked

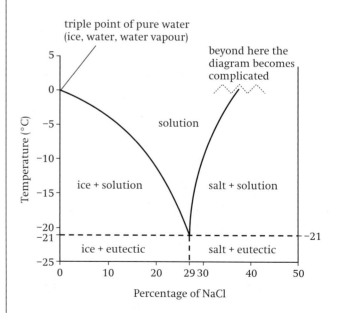

● **Figure 2.18** Part of the phase diagram for mixtures of sodium chloride and water, showing the triple point, the solidus and the various regions that occur. The pressure is (approximately) 100 kPa. (Note that the diagram is not drawn to scale.)

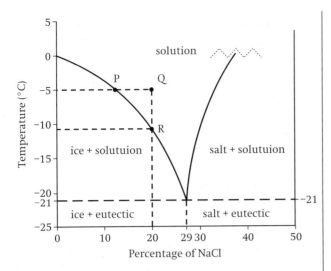

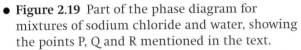

- **Figure 2.19** Part of the phase diagram for mixtures of sodium chloride and water, showing the points P, Q and R mentioned in the text.

- **Figure 2.20** This snow plough also spreads salt to help clear snow and ice from a blocked road.

at earlier in this chapter. There is separation of a eutectic mixture at −21 °C, with the eutectic containing 29% of sodium chloride. Shortly you will find that the form of the phase diagram is linked to some interesting effects in everyday life.

It is important that you realise that, like all the other phase diagrams, this one is a summary of many observations made in a series of experiments. For example, suppose you took a solution of salt and water containing 20% of salt at room temperature and slowly cooled the mixture. You would see ice begin to separate at about −10 °C. This is when the system reaches point R on the phase diagram shown in *figure 2.19*. However, the entire mixture would only solidify at −21 °C, the eutectic temperature.

Keeping the temperature constant

Now think about what would happen if you had a mixture of about 10% salt in water and the temperature was *held constant* at −5 °C. At these conditions, the system would lie at point P on the phase diagram in *figure 2.19*. Here there would be ice and solution in equilibrium. What, then, would happen if we added salt to the mixture? Some salt will dissolve in the solution, and this increases the percentage of salt in it. Let us assume that the new solution contains about 20%

salt. Remember that we have assumed that the temperature has been fixed at −5 °C, so we arrive at point Q on the phase diagram. But at this point, solid ice is *not* in equilibrium with the solution (we are not on one of the equilibrium lines): only the solution can exist in equilibrium at this point. Therefore the ice that was present at P will dissolve.

If you have understood this, you should now also understand why it is that, if there is a danger of frost, salt is spread on roads in winter (*figure 2.20*). The atmosphere holds the temperature constant (or nearly so), and adding the salt causes any ice to melt, thus reducing the chances of accidents occurring.

Allowing the temperature to change

Let us return to our (imaginary) solution at point P in *figure 2.19*; but this time we shall not keep the temperature constant. Instead, it will be allowed to change in accord with how the system changes. Imagine that we put water in a thermos flask, and initially we lowered the temperature to −5 °C. If we do not allow equilibrium to be achieved, there will be both ice and water in the flask. Now suppose we added salt to the flask. The system will change until all three can exist together at equilibrium. There is only one place that this can happen – at the eutectic point. Here the temperature will be −21 °C. In other words, by adding salt to the ice and water mixture, the temperature will immediately start to fall, and not stop until −21 °C (assuming the system is allowed to reach equilibrium – and this may take a considerable time).

Notice that the system achieves this feat without us having to do anything except add salt. The effect has been known for very many years, and a salt/ice/water mixture is known as freezing mixture. You might like to try the experiment by making up a such a mixture yourself at home.

SAQ 2.7

What connection do you think 'freezing mixture' might have with the history of ice itself, and ice cream?

SUMMARY

◆ A phase has the same physical and chemical composition in all its parts.

◆ The pairs of pressure and temperature readings that make the lines on a phase diagram are all found from experiment.

◆ The lines on a phase diagram represent the equilibria between the various phases as vapour pressure and temperature vary.

◆ The regions between the lines on a phase diagram are labelled with the names of the phases (solid, liquid and gas) that can be in equilibrium with each other.

◆ There are two important points on a phase diagram:
  – The triple point gives the only set of conditions at which all three phases can be in equilibrium.
  – The critical point gives the temperature above which it is impossible to liquefy a gas, and where separate phases (liquid and vapour) become indistinguishable.

◆ The phase diagram of water is unusual because the line for the ice/water equilibrium slopes 'backwards'. This is a result of the hydrogen bonding in ice making ice less dense than (liquid) water.

◆ The triple point of water comes at 0.06 kPa and 273.16 K. Only then can ice, water and water vapour all be in equilibrium.

◆ The critical point of water is at 21 830 kPa and 647.4 K. Above 647.4 K it is impossible to turn water vapour into liquid water.

◆ The cooling curve for a single substance typically shows three regions corresponding to: (i) the liquid cooling (fairly steep slope); (ii) the solid separating (a horizontal line where the temperature stays constant); and (iii) the solid cooling (a gentle slope).

◆ The shape of the cooling curve for a mixture depends on the composition of the mixture (see figure 2.12 on page 24). Typically there are four parts to the curve: (i) liquid mixture cooling (fairly steep slope); (ii) solid separating from the liquid (less steep); (iii) eutectic mixture separates as a solid (horizontal line); and (iv) solid eutectic and other solid cooling (a gentle slope).

◆ A eutectic mixture has: (i) a sharp melting point like a pure substance; (ii) the lowest melting point of all the possible mixtures of the components; (iii) a cooling curve like a pure substance; and (iv) no simple formula, and is not a compound.

◆ The way the atoms are arranged in an alloy of a metal changes the way the metal crystal behaves. The additional atoms can, for example, prevent the metal crystal from fracturing so easily.

◆ An alloy, for example solder, has a lower melting point than the pure metals from which it is made.

◆ The solubility curve for sodium chloride (NaCl) in water is almost a straight line.

◆ The phase diagram for mixtures of salt and water shows that the freezing point of a salt solution is below the freezing point of pure water. Use is made of this fact when roads are treated with salt in winter to prevent ice forming.

Questions

1 How does an increase in pressure affect the melting point of solid carbon dioxide?

2 Under what conditions can the solid, liquid and vapour phases of carbon dioxide exist together at equilibrium?

3 Suppose carbon dioxide is kept in a closed container. What would you see in the container:
  a at 217 K and 2000 kPa
  b at 298 K and 6000 kPa?

4 What are the conditions at which the solid, liquid and gaseous phases of water can be at equilibrium in contact with each other?

5 Suppose we placed some water in a flask, and kept the water at 25 °C. Now imagine that we reduced the pressure inside the flask. At what pressure would you predict that the water would boil (even though it is still at 25 °C)?

6 What is the reason why ice is less dense than liquid water?

7 Suggest an explanation of why the melting point of carbon dioxide increases with pressure, while that of ice decreases with pressure.

8 Why is it that the boiling point of water is so high compared to those of other molecules of a similar mass? For example, compare water's boiling point with that of carbon dioxide.
[$M(H_2O) = 18\,g\,mol^{-1}$, $M(CO_2) = 44\,g\,mol^{-1}$]

9 Use the data shown in the table on the melting point of various mixtures of cadmium and zinc to answer the questions that follow.
  a Plot a melting point–composition diagram from the data given.

Zn in mixture (%)	Melting point (°C)
0	321
10	295
17	270
20	280
30	305
40	325
50	345
60	360
70	375
80	390
90	405
100	419

  b Sketch the cooling curve that would be obtained if a mixture containing 60% of zinc were cooled from 400 °C to room temperature.
  c What would be left in the solid obtained at the end of the experiment?

10 Do the values in *table 2.3* tell you how fast each of the solids will dissolve in water?

11 We have said that, if the solubility of a solid is to be measured at a given temperature, the solution must be saturated. Your task in this question is to outline a method of measuring the solubility of sodium chloride at room temperature. You will need to think about the definition of solubility, what equipment you will have to use, and what measurements you will need to make. Write down the main steps of the method you decide upon. You might find it helpful to discuss this question with another student and decide on a joint answer. (By the way, you won't be asked how to measure solubilities in your examinations.)

CHAPTER 3

Distribution between phases

By the end of this chapter you should be able to:

1 describe and explain how the *solubility of a gas* in a liquid is affected by pressure, temperature and change of chemical state;

2 state *Henry's law* and apply it in simple calculations;

3 state what is meant by a *partition coefficient*;

4 calculate a partition coefficient for a system in which the solute is in the same molecular state in the two solutions;

5 explain *solvent extraction*.

The solubility of gases in water

In the previous chapter we discussed the solubility of salts, such as sodium chloride, in water. However, gases can also dissolve in liquids. For example, you are probably familiar with the fact that it is oxygen dissolved in water that allows fish to survive in the sea, lakes and ponds (*figure 3.1*). In this chapter we shall examine the nature of gas solubilities in some detail; but for the most part we will only concern ourselves with gases dissolving in water (rather than, for example, in organic solvents such as propanone).

The first thing to say is that gases tend to separate into two types: those that are highly soluble in water, and those that are only slightly soluble. *Table 3.1* gives some examples. Those gases that are very soluble react with water rather than just dissolving in it. For example, oxygen is only slightly soluble in water, and when it dissolves in water, the oxygen remains as O_2 molecules. All

Gases that do not react significantly with water	
	Solubility (mol dm^{-3} of water)
Carbon dioxide	3.42×10^{-4}
Carbon monoxide	9.86×10^{-4}
Hydrogen	7.84×10^{-4}
Methane	1.42×10^{-3}
Nitrogen	6.57×10^{-4}
Oxygen	1.27×10^{-3}
Gases that do react with water	
	Solubility (mol dm^{-3} of water)
Ammonia	17.9
Hydrogen bromide	9.1
Hydrogen chloride	22.6
Sulphur trioxide	Too high to measure, and nature of solution changes radically

● **Table 3.1** Examples of solubilities of gases in water at 25 °C (measured when each gas is at approximately 100 kPa pressure).

● **Figure 3.1** Gases can dissolve in water. Oxygen allows fish and other marine animals to survive.

that happens is that the molecules become surrounded by water molecules. If water containing dissolved oxygen is boiled, it is possible to retrieve all the dissolved oxygen as a gas. Now compare this with hydrogen chloride. This gas is far more soluble than oxygen; indeed, the solution it makes is hydrochloric acid, and it is impossible to retrieve all the original hydrogen chloride by boiling the acid solution. The reaction taking place for hydrogen chloride is

$$HCl(g) + H_2O(l) \rightarrow H_3O^+(aq) + Cl^-(aq)$$

It is possible to make more of a fairly insoluble gas (like oxygen) dissolve by putting it under increased pressure. The pressure forces more of the molecules into the liquid. However, if the pressure is reduced, the extra gas will bubble out. A similar situation arises when champagne is opened (*figure 3.2*).

You may find it useful to know these three general rules:

1 A gas that reacts with water usually has a high solubility.
2 The solubility of a gas decreases as the temperature increases.
3 The solubility of a gas increases as the pressure of the gas increases.

● **Figure 3.2** Carbon dioxide is produced naturally by fermentation inside a bottle of champagne, and is dissolved in the liquid champagne. A fountain of champagne spray can be produced when the pressure is released by removing the cork.

In the remainder of this unit we shall only consider gases that do not react at all, or only react very slightly with water. Such gases were first investigated by William Henry in the early 1800s.

Henry's law

Henry showed that the volume of gas dissolved was proportional to the pressure of the gas. This seemingly simple observation had some important repercussions at the time, not the least of which was that it showed that gases such as nitrogen and oxygen behaved independently of one another. This fact gave support to John Dalton's atomic theory of gases. In modern terms we can state **Henry's law** in this way:

> The concentration of gas dissolved in a liquid at a constant temperature is proportional to the partial pressure of the gas.

In symbols this becomes

$$\text{concentration of dissolved gas} \propto p$$

or

$$\text{concentration of dissolved gas} = K_h p$$

where K_h is a constant, so that Henry's law can also be written in the form

$$\frac{\text{concentration of dissolved gas}}{p} = K_h$$

Note that it is the pressure of the gas itself, i.e. its **partial pressure**, that is important. For example, for hydrogen gas, we would write Henry's law as

$$\frac{[H_2(aq)]}{p_{H_2}} = 7.74 \times 10^{-6}\,\text{mol dm}^{-3}\,\text{kPa}^{-1}$$

We must be careful to decide on the units to use in applying Henry's law. The units of concentration are mol dm^{-3}. If the pressure is measured in pascals, then the units of K_h are $\text{mol dm}^{-3}\,\text{Pa}^{-1}$, or $\text{mol dm}^{-3}\,\text{kPa}^{-1}$. You will find values of Henry's law constant in *table 3.2*.

Gas	Henry's law constant $(mol\,dm^{-3}\,kPa^{-1})$
Carbon dioxide	3.37×10^{-4}
Carbon monoxide	9.73×10^{-6}
Ethane	1.86×10^{-5}
Helium	3.83×10^{-6}
Hydrogen	7.74×10^{-6}
Methane	1.40×10^{-5}
Neon	4.47×10^{-6}
Nitrogen	6.49×10^{-6}
Nitrogen monoxide	1.91×10^{-5}
Oxygen	1.26×10^{-5}
Ozone	1.03×10^{-6}

● **Table 3.2** Values of Henry's law constant for gases at 25 °C.

Worked example 1

Air contains approximately 20% oxygen and 80% nitrogen. What is the concentration of the two gases in water that is allowed to come to equilibrium with air at 25 °C and at normal atmospheric pressure (approximately 100 kPa)?

The pressure of oxygen in the mixture is known as the partial pressure of oxygen, p_{O_2}. Similarly, the partial pressure of nitrogen in the mixture is p_{N_2}. These two pressures must add up to give the total pressure, so we have

$$p_{O_2} + p_{N_2} = 100\,kPa$$

But given that oxygen makes up 20% of the air, it must contribute 20% of the total pressure. Therefore, for oxygen

$$p_{O_2} = 0.2 \times 100\,kPa = 20\,kPa$$

and, similarly, for nitrogen

$$p_{N_2} = 0.8 \times 100\,kPa = 80\,kPa$$

Using Henry's law, and the data in *table 3.2*, for oxygen

$$\frac{[O_2(aq)]}{p_{O_2}} = 1.26 \times 10^{-5}\,mol\,dm^{-3}\,kPa^{-1}$$

so,

$$[O_2(aq)] = 1.26 \times 10^{-5}\,mol\,dm^{-3}\,kPa^{-1} \times 20\,kPa$$
$$= 2.52 \times 10^{-4}\,mol\,dm^{-3}$$

Similarly, for nitrogen we find that

$$[N_2(aq)] = 6.49 \times 10^{-6}\,mol\,dm^{-3}\,kPa^{-1} \times 80\,kPa$$
$$= 5.19 \times 10^{-4}\,mol\,dm^{-3}$$

Worked example 2

Calculate the mass of oxygen and nitrogen from air that will be dissolved in 1 dm³ of water left in equilibrium with air at normal atmospheric pressure (approximately 100 kPa) at 25 °C.

To do this, we use the values calculated in *example 1* together with a knowledge of the molecular masses of the two gases. Given that from *example 1*, $[O_2(aq)] = 2.52 \times 10^{-4}\,mol\,dm^{-3}$, and that $M(O_2) = 32\,g\,mol^{-1}$, then

mass of oxygen dissolved
$$= 2.52 \times 10^{-4}\,mol\,dm^{-3} \times 32\,g\,mol^{-1}$$
$$= 0.0806\,g\,dm^{-3}$$

Similarly, with $[N_2(aq)] = 5.19 \times 10^{-4}\,mol\,dm^{-3}$ and $M(N_2) = 28\,g\,mol^{-1}$ we find that

mass of nitrogen dissolved
$$= 5.19 \times 10^{-4}\,mol\,dm^{-3} \times 28\,g\,mol^{-1}$$
$$= 0.0145\,g\,dm^{-3}$$

Worked example 3

What volume of carbon dioxide will dissolve in 10 dm³ of water kept at 25 °C in contact with the gas at 10 kPa pressure? (Assume that carbon dioxide does not react with water.)

The method here is first to use Henry's law to find the concentration of the gas in the water. Then if we know how many moles of the gas have dissolved, we can use the ideal gas equation to work out the volume of the gas under the stated conditions. We use Henry's law and the appropriate value in *table 3.2* to get

$$\frac{[CO_2(aq)]}{p_{CO_2}} = 3.37 \times 10^{-4}\,mol\,dm^{-3}\,kPa^{-1}$$

Therefore,

$$[CO_2(aq)] = 3.37 \times 10^{-4}\,mol\,dm^{-3}\,kPa^{-1} \times 10\,kPa$$
$$= 3.37 \times 10^{-3}\,mol\,dm^{-3}$$

Thus, in 10 dm³ of water there is 3.37×10^{-2} mol of the gas. Then using the ideal gas equation $PV = nRT$, or $V = nRT/P$, we have

$$V = \frac{3.37 \times 10^{-2}\,mol \times 8.314\,J\,mol^{-1}\,K^{-1} \times (273 + 25)\,K}{10 \times 10^{3}\,Pa}$$
$$= 8.35 \times 10^{-3}\,dm^{3}$$

This is a little over 8 cm³.

SAQ 3.1

Carbon dioxide is widely used in making 'fizzy drinks' (*figure 3.3*).

a Assume that the gas is at a pressure of 1000 kPa when it is introduced into the drink at 25 °C. What mass of the gas will dissolve in a one litre bottle of lemonade?

b What do you see when the bottle is opened at normal atmospheric pressure, and why does it happen?

c Now imagine that the bottle is opened and then resealed after 250 cm³ of lemonade has been drunk. Assume that the pressure of carbon dioxide in the space at the top of the bottle is 100 kPa. What mass of carbon dioxide is now dissolved in the remaining lemonade?

d What volume would the two masses of carbon dioxide take up if each volume was measured at 100 kPa pressure? (Assume that 1 mol of gas occupies 24 dm³ at 25 °C and 100 kPa pressure.)

e Estimate the mass of carbon dioxide released into the atmosphere if a group of 20 students each open 20 one litre bottles of lemonade every week for one year.

● **Figure 3.3** Bubbles of carbon dioxide in a glass of lemonade.

Miscible and immiscible liquids

Ethanol (C_2H_5OH), or 'alcohol' as it is often referred to, has a number of properties that make it one of the most widely used organic chemicals. Especially, it is the basis for all alcoholic drinks such as beers, wines and spirits. It is obvious to anyone who has seen, or drunk, an alcoholic

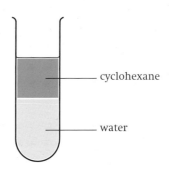

● **Figure 3.4** Cyclohexane and water are two immiscible liquids. They separate into two layers when shaken together.

drink that alcohol and water mix very easily – there are never two separate layers present. We say that alcohol and water are **miscible** liquids. This behaviour is not shown by the majority of organic liquids and water. For example, cyclohexane (C_6H_{12}) will not mix with water. It forms a totally separate layer lying on top of the water. This behaviour is common to all liquid hydrocarbons. We say that cyclohexane is **immiscible** with water (*figure 3.4*). Unfortunately, the immiscibility of water and crude or refined oil has been responsible for some horrendous examples of pollution of the sea and coastline following accidents involving oil tankers (*figure 3.5*).

Let us think about making a mixture of ethanol and water. We could take ethanol and add it to water, in which case we would say that the ethanol was dissolving in the water. On the other hand, if we added water to ethanol, we could say that the water was dissolving in the ethanol.

● **Figure 3.5** The Braer oil spill, Shetlands, Scotland. Oil and water are immiscible, but spilt oil can be dispersed more effectively by adding detergents to the oil slick.

In practice, it would not matter which method we used because ethanol and water are miscible in all proportions. In the case of two completely immiscible liquids, both are insoluble in the other.

However, there are some liquids that are partially soluble in each other. For example, suppose we took 100 g of water at 50 °C, and slowly added phenol (C_6H_5OH) at 50 °C to it. We would find that at first the phenol would dissolve quite happily. However, when the proportion of phenol gets to about 10% of the total mass of the mixture, two layers appear. In a sense, we can think of the water becoming saturated with phenol in much the same way as it does if we dissolve a solid such as salt in it. A similar change takes place if we take phenol at 50 °C and add water. At first the water dissolves, but when the proportion gets to about 20% of water, the phenol becomes saturated with water and two layers form. Phenol and water are **partially miscible** liquids at 50 °C.

SAQ 3.2

Why do water and ethanol mix? [*Hint*: Think about the intermolecular bonds that hold water molecules and ethanol molecules together in the liquid state.]

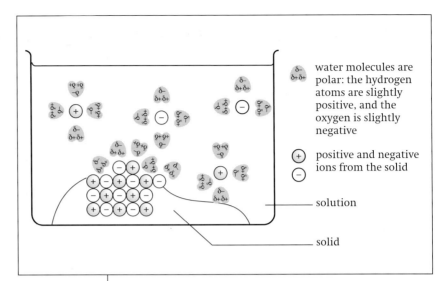

water molecules are polar: the hydrogen atoms are slightly positive, and the oxygen is slightly negative

(+) positive and negative
(−) ions from the solid

solution

solid

● **Figure 3.6** A *very* exaggerated view of how water molecules attract ions from the surface of a solid into solution, and then hold the ions in the solution. The ions are said to be **solvated** by the water molecules. The process is also helped by the fact that water is a good insulator, so once the positive and negative ions are separated, the water molecules reduce the influence of the attractive forces bringing them together.

Water will dissolve some covalent substances, but the majority that dissolve easily do so because they react with water. The others that dissolve usually can hydrogen bond with water molecules. *Table 3.3* gives examples.

SAQ 3.3

Decide which of the following statements is/are true, and which is/are false:
a Sodium chloride will dissolve in octane.
b Oxygen will dissolve in cyclohexane.
c Chlorine will dissolve in cyclohexane.
d Water and methanol will be completely miscible.
e Cyclohexane and butan-1-ol will be completely miscible.
[*Note*: You do not have to know for sure what the answer is; you only have to decide which option is most probably correct.]

Solubility rules

There is a general rule in chemistry that 'like dissolves like'. In practice, this means that:

> Covalent substances tend to mix with, or dissolve in, other covalent substances.
> Ionic substances do not mix with, or dissolve in, covalent substances (water is an exception).

As always, we should interpret rules in chemistry as being suspect – there will always be exceptions. The major one is water. Water *is* a covalent substance, but its highly polar nature makes it an excellent solvent for ionic compounds (*figure 3.6*).

The partition law

You may have used the immiscibility of cyclohexane (or some other organic liquid) with water as way of testing for the presence of iodine or bromine. The method is to shake a little

Covalent substance	Will dissolve	Which is	Because
Water	Sodium chloride, easily	Ionic	Water molecules attract the ions (see *figure 3.6*)
	Hydrogen chloride gas, easily	Covalent	HCl reacts to makes hydrochloric acid, $H^+(aq) + Cl^-(aq)$
	Oxygen gas, partially	Covalent	Instantaneous dipole forces between oxygen molecules and between water molecules mean they can attract each other; but the polar nature of water molecules tends to keep them together and prevent oxygen molecules getting between them
	Ethanol	Covalent	Hydrogen bonding can take place between ethanol and water molecules
Cyclohexane	Octane	Covalent	instantaneous dipole forces between molecules
	Iodine	Covalent	instantaneous dipole forces between molecules

● **Table 3.3** Examples of solubilities.

cyclohexane with an aqueous solution in which iodine is thought to be present. (An **aqueous solution** is one that is made of a substance dissolved in water.) If iodine is there, the colour of the cyclohexane layer changes from clear to purple (*figure 3.7*). Iodine molecules happen to be much more soluble in cyclohexane than in water, so they collect in the cyclohexane, giving the characteristic colour change.

However, not all the iodine in the lower aqueous layer will dissolve in the cyclohexane. Provided the two layers are left in contact with each other for sufficiently long, and the temperature is kept constant, an equilibrium is set up between iodine molecules entering and leaving the two layers. At equilibrium

$$\frac{\text{rate of iodine molecules}}{\text{leaving the aqueous layer}} = \frac{\text{rate of iodine molecules}}{\text{leaving the cyclohexane layer}}$$

and then the concentrations of iodine in each layer are constant, and the ratio of the concentrations is constant. Whenever there is an equilibrium in chemistry, there is an associated equilibrium constant. In this case it is called the **partition coefficient**. We shall give it the symbol, K_{pc}. In this case we have

$$K_{pc} = \frac{\text{concentration of iodine in cyclohexane}}{\text{concentration of iodine in water}}$$

In general, for a solute that is in contact with two solvents we can write the **partition law** as:

$$K_{pc} = \frac{\text{concentration of solute in first solvent}}{\text{concentration of solute in second solvent}}$$

(The decision about which is the first solvent, and which is the second, is made so as to make the value of K_{pc} as large as possible, e.g. $K_{pc} = 99$, rather than putting the values the other way round and making $K_{pc} = 1/99 = 0.0101$, as such small values are less easy to use.)

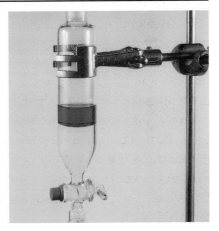

● **Figure 3.7** In water/cyclohexane iodine turns the upper cyclohexane layer purple (dark in this photo).

Now we shall look at an example calculation using the partition law.

Worked example 4

A solution contained 1 g of iodine dissolved in $40\,cm^3$ of aqueous potassium iodide. If we shook this solution with $20\,cm^3$ of tetrachloromethane, what mass of iodine would be transferred into the tetrachloromethane? (Tetrachloromethane is an organic liquid, also known as carbon tetrachloride, that has been used as a dry cleaning fluid. It has a very harmful vapour and is no longer widely available.)

To answer this, we need to know that the partition coefficient between tetrachloromethane and water is 85 at 25 °C:

$$\frac{\text{concentration of iodine in tetrachloromethane}}{\text{concentration of iodine in aqueous solution}} = 85$$

Let us say that x grams of iodine go into the tetrachloromethane. This will leave $(1 - x)$ grams of iodine in the aqueous layer. Then we have

concentration of iodine in tetrachloromethane

$$= x/20 \, \text{g cm}^{-3}$$

concentration of iodine in aqueous solution

$$= (1 - x)/40 \, \text{g cm}^{-3}$$

Therefore,

$$\frac{x/20}{(1 - x)/40} = 85$$

$$\frac{x}{20} \div \frac{(1 - x)}{40} = 85$$

$$\frac{x}{20} \times \frac{40}{(1 - x)} = 85$$

$$\frac{2x}{(1 - x)} = 85$$

$$2x = 85(1 - x)$$

$$2x = 85 - 85x$$

$$87x = 85$$

which gives

$$x = \frac{85}{87} = 0.9770$$

This tells us that we should have 0.9770 g of iodine in the tetrachloromethane, with 0.0230 g of iodine left in the aqueous layer. (We need to work to four significant figures here because we shall use these values in SAQ 3.4.)

If we wanted to collect the iodine, we would have to evaporate the tetrachloromethane carefully. [*Safety note*: This organic liquid is carcinogenic, so don't try this yourself!]

Partition experiments are extremely important in the pharmaceutical industry and in studies of the environment. The solvent that is widely used is another organic liquid called octan-1-ol (or sometimes 1-octanol, or just octanol), $C_8H_{17}OH$. The partition coefficients for a very large number of organic compounds dissolving in it in contact with water have been measured. For example, thousands of tonnes of the compound dichloromethane CH_2Cl_2 (known in industry as methylene chloride) are produced every year. The

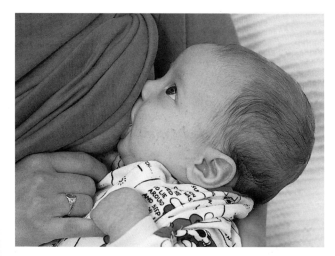

● **Figure 3.8** Breast milk can contain traces of organic pollutants.

compound has many uses, one of which is as a paint stripper; unfortunately, it is also a highly persistent and dangerous pollutant – it can cause cancer. One way to determine its concentration in a sample of water is to do a partition experiment with octan-1-ol. (See question 9 at the end of this chapter.)

Octan-1-ol is also used to extract molecules from naturally occurring liquids. For example, the milk of nursing mothers (*figure 3.8*) has been analysed to show that breast milk can be contaminated as a result of the mother breathing in fumes of organic liquids such as dichloromethane.

Solvent extraction

You now know that it is possible to extract some of a solute in a solution by shaking with another liquid in which the solute is more soluble. This is the basis of solvent extraction; i.e. separating a substance from a mixture by using its ability to dissolve to different extents in different solvents. When you answer SAQ 3.4, you should discover that more iodine could be removed from the original solution by shaking with two separate 20 cm^3 portions of tetrachloromethane rather than by shaking with one 40 cm^3 portion. This is a general rule in solvent extraction:

> Repeated extractions with smaller volumes of solvent are more efficient than one extraction with a larger volume.

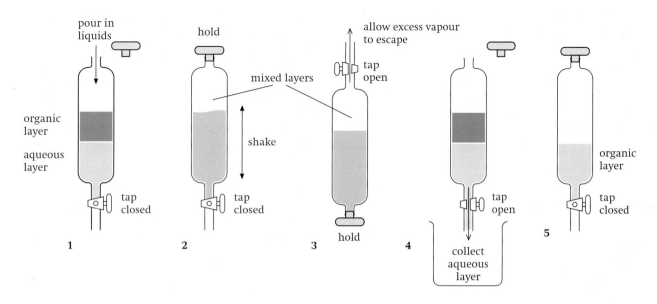

- **Figure 3.9** A separating funnel can be used for solvent extraction. The steps are as follows:
1 Add the aqueous and organic liquids to the separating funnel.
2 With the stopper in, shake the two liquids together.
3 Occasionally turn the funnel upside down, making sure that the stopper remains in place. Open the tap to allow excess vapour to be released. Close the tap.
4 Turn the separating funnel the 'right' way up. Allow the liquids to separate, and run off the lower, aqueous, layer.
5 Keep the organic layer for further treatment.
Note: It is important not to shake the liquids too vigorously, because, if the droplets become too small, they take a long time to separate into layers again.
Safety note: Always wear safety glasses if you do this experiment, and never point the funnel at yourself or another student.

However, no matter how many times an extraction is done, there will always be a tiny amount of the solute left in the original solution. This is because it is impossible to move an equilibrium completely (100%) to one side or the other.

You might like to look at *figure 3.9*, which shows you a way of carrying out a solvent extraction.

SAQ 3.4

Using the same data as in *Worked example 4* on pages 37–8, suppose that the remaining aqueous layer was separated after the first extraction of iodine.
a This layer was then extracted with another 20 cm³ of tetrachloromethane. What mass of iodine would have been left in the aqueous layer after the two extractions?
b If the original aqueous iodine solution had just been shaken with 40 cm³ of tetrachloromethane, what mass of iodine would have been extracted?
c Is it best to extract the iodine with two smaller volumes or one larger volume of solvent?

SAQ 3.5

Suppose that 50 cm³ of a 0.1 moldm⁻³ solution of iodine in potassium iodide was shaken with 10 cm³ of an organic liquid. The partition coefficient between the organic liquid and water was 100.

Use the correct version of the partition law (see *Worked example 4* above) to calculate:
a the concentration of iodine in the organic layer at equilibrium;
b the mass of iodine in the organic layer at equilibrium; and
c the mass of iodine left in the aqueous layer. You will need to know that $M(I_2) = 254 \, \text{g mol}^{-1}$.
[*Hint*: The safest way to do this problem is to work in terms of the number of moles of iodine in a given volume of liquid.]

SUMMARY

- The solubilities of gases in water follows these rules:
  - A gas that reacts with water usually has a high solubility.
  - The solubility decreases as the temperature increases.
  - The solubility increases as the pressure of the gas increases.

- Henry's law states that: The concentration of gas dissolved in a liquid at a constant temperature is proportional to the partial pressure (p) of the gas.

- In symbols Henry's law is

  $$\frac{[\text{gas}]}{p_{\text{gas}}} = K_{\text{h}}$$

  where K_{h} is Henry's law constant. Like all equilibrium constants K_{h} is a constant at a given temperature.

- Immiscible liquids do not mix, and form two layers when put together.

- A partition coefficient is an equilibrium constant that describes the ratio in which a solute will be distributed between two immiscible liquids in contact with one another. The general formula for the partition coefficient is

  $$K_{\text{pc}} = \frac{\text{concentration of solute in first solvent}}{\text{concentration of solute in second solvent}}$$

- Solvent extraction can be used to separate a substance that dissolves more in one of a pair of immiscible liquids than in the other; for example, iodine preferentially dissolves in cyclohexane rather than in aqueous potassium iodide, so cyclohexane can be used to extract iodine from the aqueous solution.

Questions

1 In *table 3.1* on page 32 you will see that the solubility of sulphur trioxide in water is listed as being too high to measure. Find out what is made when this gas dissolves in water.

2 Ammonia is also listed in *table 3.1* as a very soluble gas. The solution it makes is sometimes called ammonium hydroxide, and given the formula NH_4OH. In fact, there is very little NH_4OH in a solution of ammonia, and the solution is best called 'aqueous ammonia' – it simply contains very large amounts of ammonia dissolved in, rather than reacted with, the water.
   a What types of intermolecular force can exist in water, and in ammonia?
   b Why would you expect ammonia and water to mix easily (i.e. why would you expect ammonia to be very soluble in water)?

3 In the table below, there is a set of data showing the solubility of carbon dioxide in water at 25 °C for a range of pressures of the gas. Plot a graph of the results, and use the graph to estimate a value for the Henry's law constant for carbon dioxide.

Partial pressure of CO_2 (kPa)	Solubility (mol dm^{-3})
5	1.72×10^{-3}
10	3.44×10^{-3}
20	6.83×10^{-3}
30	1.03×10^{-2}
40	1.37×10^{-2}
50	1.71×10^{-2}
100	3.41×10^{-2}

(Data taken from *Handbook of Physics and Chemistry*, 70th edn, CRC Press, 1995.)

4 When fizzy drinks are left open to the atmosphere, they go 'flat'.

a What volume of carbon dioxide would be found in one litre of soda water that is left open at 25 °C for many hours when the atmospheric pressure is 100 kPa?

b What would be the volume if the carbon dioxide were removed from the water and its volume measured at 100 kPa pressure?
[*Note*: You will need to know that carbon dioxide makes up about 0.03% of the atmosphere.]

5 Why, in question 4, did it say that the soda water was to be left 'for many hours'?

6 In *table 3.3* on page 37 there is no entry for an ionic substance dissolving another substance. What do you think might be the reason for this omission (apart from the author being lazy perhaps!)?

7 When iodine is used in solution, e.g. as a test for starch, it is not just iodine itself that is present in water. Pure iodine is almost completely insoluble in water. However, it dissolves very easily if iodide ions are present, because an equilibrium is set up between iodine molecules and triiodide ions, I_3^-. The latter ions are very soluble in water, but are insoluble in organic solvents. These ions also give a dark brown colour to the solution. However, iodine *is* soluble in organic solvents such as cyclohexane, or another called 1,1,1-trichloroethane. When iodine is present as separate molecules, it has a lilac/purple colour. The equation for the equilibrium is:

$$I_2(s) \quad + \quad I^-(aq) \quad \rightleftharpoons \quad I_3^-(aq)$$
insoluble in water, soluble in 1,1,1-trichloroethane   soluble in water, insoluble in 1,1,1-trichloroethane

Use this information to describe carefully what you would see and what happens in terms of the equilibria involved when iodine solution is shaken with 1,1,1-trichloroethane.

8 How many times do you think an extraction should be done in order to remove 100% of the iodine from iodine dissolved in potassium iodide solution?

9 After stripping paint from a window frame, imagine that you washed in water a brush containing dichloromethane (methylene chloride). Assume that 250 cm^3 of the washings was taken and used in a partition experiment with 100 cm^3 octan-1-ol. It was found that 3.3 g of dichloromethane went into the octan-1-ol layer. Also, 0.46 g was found in the washings.

a What was the concentration of dichloromethane in the octan-1-ol?

b What was the concentration of dichloromethane in the washings?

c What is the value of the partition coefficient for dichloromethane between octan-1-ol and water?

d Not all the dichloromethane on the brush dissolved in the water – where else did it go?

CHAPTER 4

Raoult's law and distillation

By the end of this chapter you should be able to:

1 state and apply *Raoult's law;*

2 explain qualitatively the *effect of a non-volatile solute* on the vapour pressure of a solvent and on the freezing point and boiling point of the solution;

3 outline, in qualitative terms, the relationships of boiling point and enthalpy change of vaporisation with intermolecular forces;

4 interpret the boiling point–composition curves for mixtures of two miscible liquids in terms of (i) 'ideal' behaviour and (ii) positive or negative deviations from Raoult's law, related to intermolecular attractions or bonding;

5 describe the principles of *fractional distillation* of ideal liquid mixtures;

6 describe a typical laboratory *fractionating column;*

7 demonstrate a knowledge and understanding of the packing of fractionating columns and other means of establishing equilibrium at different temperatures between liquid and vapour;

8 explain the concept of *theoretical plates* in fractionating columns;

9 deduce the number of theoretical plates by graphical means, using given data;

10 understand and use the term *azeotropic mixture;*

11 explain the limitations on separating two components that form an azeotropic mixture;

12 explain *steam distillation* of two immiscible liquids;

13 demonstrate an awareness of the applications of fractional and steam distillation to the separation of the components of liquid mixtures.

Effects of non-volatile solutes

In this chapter we are going to study distillation. Distillation is one of the key processes used in chemistry – in individual laboratories and on a very large scale in industry (*figure 4.1*). Huge volumes of whisky, gin, vodka and other alcoholic drinks are made using distillation. Also, the world relies on the distillation of crude oil to produce petrol and other fuels for cars, planes, lorries and the like. However, before we can understand how distillation works, we need to know rather more about how mixtures of solids and liquids behave.

So, we shall begin with a review of how the vapour pressure and boiling point of a liquid change when another substance is dissolved in it.

In chapter 2 we saw how the presence of salt in water influenced the vapour pressure of water above the solution. Salt is an example of a non-volatile solute. (You won't find particles of solid salt 'evaporating' from a solution!) Because the water molecules are strongly attracted to the positively charged sodium ions and negatively charged chloride ions, the water molecules tend

● **Figure 4.1** Oil refining and whisky production both rely on the process of distillation.

to be more tightly held in the solution; so the vapour pressure above the solution goes down. You might like to look back at the phase diagram for salt and water that was drawn in *figure 2.18* on page 28. This shows that the freezing point of a salt solution is reduced below that of pure water. Also, the boiling point of salt water is above that of pure water. In a simple way you can think of this being the result of needing to put more energy into the solution to drag the water molecules away from the sodium and chloride ions and turn the liquid into vapour.

To summarise, we can say that, compared to a pure solvent, the presence of a non-volatile solute tends to:

1 depress the freezing point, and
2 raise the boiling point.

Vapour pressures and Raoult's law

Changes in vapour pressure do not only happen when ionic solids dissolve in water. Changes occur even when the solute happens to be another liquid; i.e. when liquids mix, the vapour pressure of each liquid changes compared to the value of the pure liquid. *Figure 4.2* shows how the vapour pressures of hexane and heptane vary as the proportions of the two liquids in a mixture are changed. (A mixture that shows such a straight line graph is called an ideal mixture – see next subsection.)

One way of summarising the way the proportions of the liquids change in a mixture is to state their mole fractions. (You will find more information about mole fractions in *Chemistry 2*, page 127.) If we have two liquids, A and B, we can write the number of moles of A as n_A and the number of moles of B as n_B. The **mole fractions** of each are:

$$\text{mole fraction of A, } N_A = \frac{n_A}{n_A + n_B}$$

$$\text{mole fraction of B, } N_B = \frac{n_B}{n_A + n_B}$$

You can see from *figure 4.2* that the vapour pressures of the two liquids are directly proportional to their mole fractions in the mixture (the vapour pressure plots are straight lines). Thus, for example, if we doubled the mole fraction of hexane in the mixture, the vapour pressure of hexane above

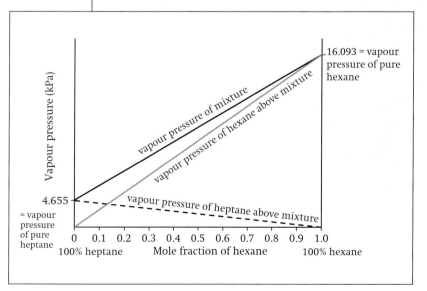

● **Figure 4.2** Vapour pressure–composition diagram for a mixture of hexane and heptane.

● **Figure 4.3**
François-Marie Raoult,
1830–1901

the mixture would also double. We can put this relation between mole fraction and vapour pressure in symbols by writing

$$p_A = N_A \times p_A^{\circ} \quad \text{and} \quad p_B = N_B \times p_B^{\circ}$$

where p_A° and p_B° are the vapour pressures of pure A and pure B.

These two equations are a mathematical statement of a law first stated in 1886 by the French scientist François-Marie Raoult (*figure 4.3*). In modern terms **Raoult's law** says:

> The vapour pressure of a solvent in a solution is equal to the vapour pressure of the pure solvent multiplied by its mole fraction in the solution.

SAQ 4.1

The formulae of hexane and heptane are C_6H_{14} and C_7H_{16}, respectively. A mixture was made containing 17.2 g of hexane and 30 g of heptane.

a What was the mole fraction of each hydrocarbon in the mixture?

b Given that the vapour pressures of pure hexane and of pure heptane are approximately 16.1 kPa and 4.7 kPa, respectively, at 25 °C, what would be the vapour pressures of the two liquids above the mixture at 25 °C?

c What would be the total vapour pressure of the mixture?

d Is the vapour above the mixture richer in hexane or in heptane?

e Which liquid would you expect to have the lower boiling point?

Ideal and non-ideal solutions

There are not many liquids that obey Raoult's law irrespective of the proportions in which they are mixed. Those mixtures that *do* obey Raoult's law are called **ideal solutions**, or **ideal mixtures**. As we said earlier, *figure 4.2* shows that a mixture of hexane and heptane is an ideal solution (or ideal mixture). The majority of liquid mixtures *do not* give straight line graphs when their vapour pressures are plotted against their mole fractions. A mixture of ethanol and water is an example; but there are many others that also show non-ideal behaviour. We say that solutions such as ethanol and water show *deviations* from ideal behaviour:

1 In some cases the vapour pressures of the liquids in the mixture are *greater* than would be expected from the law – these mixtures are said to show **positive deviations** from Raoult's law.

2 For other mixtures the vapour pressures are *less* than predicted by the law – such mixtures are said to show **negative deviations** from Raoult's law.

Often, deviations from Raoult's law are found with liquids that have hydrogen bonding between their molecules.

The most common types of vapour pressure diagram are shown in *figure 4.4*. In this figure (and all vapour pressure diagrams of mixtures), the series of points on the heavy full line that are found from experiment are the sums of the vapour pressures of the liquids in the mixture. For a mixture of two liquids A and B, we can write this in symbols as

$$P_{mix} = P_A + P_B$$

Examples of both ideal mixtures and non-ideal mixtures are given in *table 4.1*.

Mixture	Behaviour
Hexane + heptane	Ideal
Benzene + methylbenzene	Ideal
Methanol + water	Negative deviation
Trichloromethane + propanone	Negative deviation, with a minimum
Ethanol + water	Positive deviation, with a maximum

● **Table 4.1** Liquid mixtures and Raoult's law.

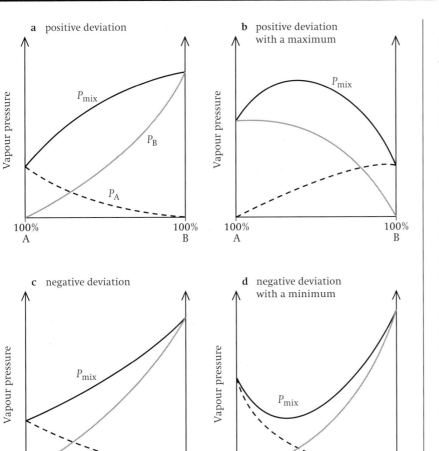

a positive deviation

P_{mix}

P_B

P_A

100% A   100% B

b positive deviation with a maximum

P_{mix}

100% A   100% B

c negative deviation

P_{mix}

100% A   100% B

d negative deviation with a minimum

P_{mix}

100% A   100% B

● **Figure 4.4** The four types of deviation from Raoult's law. Each full graph line P_{mix} corresponds to readings taken at constant temperature. Actually, when the mixtures contain very little of one liquid dissolved in a great deal of the other (e.g. 99.99% A and 0.01% B), the graphs do become linear; i.e. very dilute solutions (mixtures) do obey Raoult's law.

Why are there deviations from Raoult's law?

First, let us understand why a mixture of hexane and heptane makes an ideal solution. You should be able to see that the more hexane (or heptane) molecules there are in the mixture, the more likely it is that molecules of hexane (or heptane) will escape into the vapour. Therefore, we would expect the vapour pressure of hexane (or heptane) to increase as its mole fraction increases. This is what Raoult's law claims for an ideal solution. However, this line of argument only works because:

1 the forces between hexane molecules are instantaneous dipole forces,

2 the forces between heptane molecules are instantaneous dipole forces, *and*

3 the forces between hexane and heptane molecules are also instantaneous dipole forces.

This means that if you were a hexane molecule it matters little whether you are surrounded by other hexane molecules or by heptane molecules: the forces holding you in the liquid are approximately the same, with respect to both their type and their strength.

Similarly, if you were a water molecule surrounded by other water molecules, you would be able to hydrogen bond to your nearest neighbours. But if you were to find yourself surrounded by hexane molecules, it would be impossible to make hydrogen bonds. Likewise, it would be hard for a non-polar hexane molecule to be attracted to a highly polar water molecule. In short, hexane and water molecules have nothing to gain by splitting apart from one another and joining with the 'opposing camp'. Indeed, we know that water and hexane separate into two layers when they are put together, i.e. they are completely immiscible.

A mixture of ethanol and water is a less extreme case. Ethanol molecules can hydrogen bond together, just as can water molecules. This is why ethanol and water mix easily, i.e. they are completely miscible. However, experiment shows that the vapour pressure above a mixture of ethanol and water is greater than that predicted from Raoult's law. A mixture of ethanol and water shows a *positive deviation* from the law. That is, the molecules in the mixture have a greater tendency to escape than in the pure liquids. This is because the strength of the bonding between the two different types of molecule is less than in the pure liquids.

As you go through this chapter, you will find other examples of mixtures that show deviations from Raoult's law; indeed, very few mixtures obey his law exactly.

SAQ 4.2

Would you expect a mixture of
a hexane and pentane;
b propan-1-ol and water;
to show deviations from Raoult's law?

How to interpret vapour pressure diagrams

You will find that it can be useful to show two lines on a vapour pressure diagram. One of the lines shows how the vapour pressure changes with the composition of the liquid mixture. This is the line we have already drawn on the diagrams. The second line shows how the composition of the *vapour* changes. The two lines are different because:

> The vapour is always richer in the more volatile component.

That is, the composition of the vapour is usually different from that of the solution from which it came. *Figure 4.5* shows you typical shapes of the two lines for non-ideal mixtures. The diagrams tell us the composition of the liquid and vapour that are *in equilibrium* with each other at a particular vapour pressure and temperature.

Example 1 – positive deviation

In *figure 4.5a*, at the vapour pressure *p*, the vapour has composition given by C and the liquid has composition D. If you look at the composition scale, you can see that the vapour contains more of the less volatile component, A, than does the liquid. (The less volatile component has the lower vapour pressure.)

Example 2 – negative deviation with a minimum

Look at *figure 4.5d*, which shows the typical shape of a vapour pressure diagram for a mixture showing a negative deviation from Raoult's law, and that has a minimum in the graph. There are two liquid mixtures (compositions R and S) that can have a vapour pressure *p*, and these two mixtures have vapours of different compositions: for the liquid of composition R, its vapour would have composition Q; and for the liquid with composition S, its vapour would have composition T.

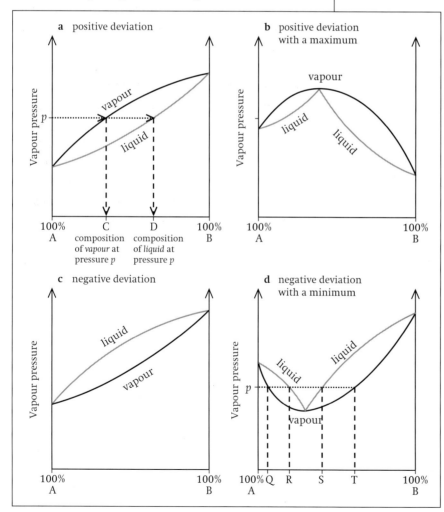

● **Figure 4.5** When there is **a** a positive or **b** a negative deviation from Raoult's law, the liquid mixture has a different composition from the vapour above it. See the text for a brief discussion of two examples.

Boiling points

Boiling points and intermolecular forces

A reliable rule about boiling points and intermolecular forces in a liquid (or mixture of liquids) is that:

> The higher the boiling point, the stronger the intermolecular forces.

Evidence for this claim comes from examining the heats of vaporisation of liquids. One way of highlighting the differences between liquids is to look at the energy required to vaporise unit mass of each liquid at its boiling point. *Table 4.2* illustrates some typical values of the heats of vaporisation, ΔH_{vap}, in kJ mol^{-1}. The values are directly related to the type of intermolecular bonding in the liquids. For example, pentane, hexane and benzene have no hydrogen bonding, and their ΔH_{vap} values are smaller than those of water, methanol and ethanol, which all have hydrogen bonding.

The way that heats of vaporisation vary with boiling point can be complicated, but a reasonable rule is that, as boiling point increases, heats of vaporisation increase. The data in *table 4.2* illustrate the 'rule'. Especially, where there is strong hydrogen bonding, you will find high boiling points and high values of the heat of vaporisation.

The boiling points of mixtures

Distillation is a method of separating mixtures of miscible liquids. There are three key ideas that

Liquid	Boiling pt (°C)	ΔH_{vap} (kJ mol^{-1})
Pentane	36	13
Hexane	69	23
Benzene	80	32
Water	100	41
Methanol	65	35
Ethanol	78	39

● **Table 4.2** Heats of vaporisation of some liquids.

you must know if you are to understand how and why distillation works (the third follows from the first two):

1. A liquid boils when its vapour pressure equals the atmospheric pressure.
2. The higher the vapour pressure of a liquid, the more volatile is the liquid.
3. A liquid with a high vapour pressure will boil at a lower temperature than a liquid with a lower vapour pressure.

The importance of these ideas is that we can use vapour pressure diagrams to tell us how the boiling point of a mixture of liquids will change as the composition of the mixture changes. Instead of plotting vapour pressure against composition, we can plot boiling point against composition. This is done for an ideal mixture in *figure 4.6*. If you compare the diagrams in the figure, you can see that, where the line goes up on a vapour pressure diagram, the line goes down on the boiling point diagram (and vice versa). This has the effect

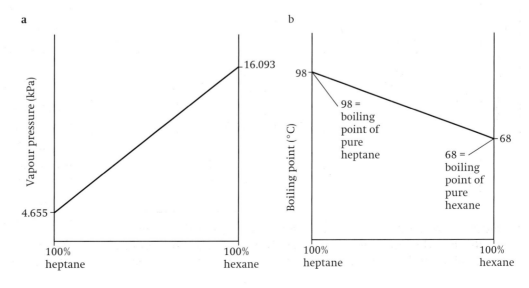

● **Figure 4.6** For an ideal mixture of hexane and heptane, the vapour pressure–composition diagram (**a**) slopes in the opposite direction to the boiling point–composition diagram (**b**). (Low vapour pressure means high boiling point, and vice versa.)

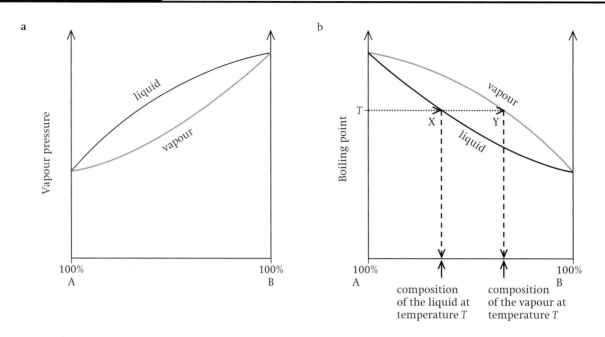

● **Figure 4.7 a** Vapour pressure–composition and **b** boiling point–composition diagrams for a mixture showing a negative deviation from Raoult's law. It is important to move across the boiling point–composition diagram at a given temperature. At the temperature *T*, the liquid mixture X is in equilibrium with vapour Y. Notice that Y is richer in the component (B) that has the lower boiling point (so is more volatile).

of turning the liquid and vapour composition lines upside down. The corresponding diagrams for non-ideal mixtures are more complicated, but the same general point holds. For example, *figure 4.7* gives an example of a non-ideal mixture showing a negative deviation from Raoult's law. *Figure 4.7a* shows the vapour pressure curves, and *figure 4.7b* shows the corresponding boiling point diagram. Notice that, again, a low vapour pressure indicates a high boiling point (and vice versa).

There is a right and a wrong way of interpreting a boiling point diagram:

> The right way to interpret a boiling point diagram is to start on the temperature axis and work across.

If we do this as shown in *figure 4.7b*, starting at temperature *T*, we meet the liquid line at X. Going further to the right, we meet the vapour line at Y. The link between the points X and Y means that:

> A liquid with composition X will be in equilibrium with a vapour of composition Y at the temperature *T*.

You can see that the vapour is richer in the more volatile component (the one with the lower boiling point).

It is wise to remember that a negative deviation from Raoult's law curves *upwards* on a boiling point diagram (see *figure 4.7*). (This is the opposite direction to that on a vapour pressure diagram.) Likewise, a mixture showing a positive deviation from Raoult's law will have a vapour line that dips *downwards* on a boiling point diagram. Finally, do be careful with boiling point diagrams; if you move upwards instead of across the diagram, you will get into a muddle.

Distillation

We are now going to explain how distillation works. Distillation is one of the most important ways of separating mixtures of chemicals into their components. For example, the everyday lives of people in rich countries depend on a ready supply of petrol for motor vehicles – and petrol is obtained by the distillation of crude oil. Much of the alcoholic drinks industry relies on distillation to concentrate ethanol from dilute solutions into

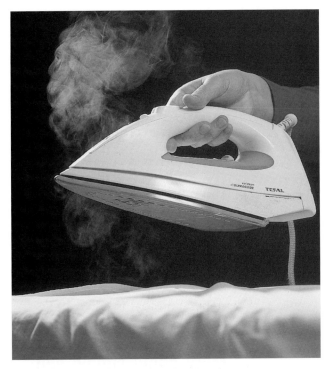

● **Figure 4.8** Distilled water contains no dissolved solids. This gives it many uses, both in the home and in the laboratory.

drinks such as whisky, gin and brandy. Distilled water is used for many every-day purposes (*figure 4.8*) as well as in the laboratory. Many schools and colleges make their own distilled water by running a simple distillation apparatus on a semi-continuous process. However, deionised water can also be made easily and used instead of distilled water.

The scales of the separation problem for distillation in the laboratory and in industry are rather different. In the laboratory, we might want to separate 20 cm^3 of one liquid from 50 cm^3 of another, and we would usually use the glass apparatus shown in *figure 4.9* for simple distillations, and the apparatus of *figure 4.10* (overleaf) for fractional distillations. (We will consider both varieties in more detail later.) Such glass apparatus may cost some tens of pounds. On an industrial scale, it can be necessary to separate many thousands of litres of a mixture into its component parts. An industrial distillation unit will probably be constructed of steel and cost hundreds of thousands of pounds, and be just one part of an entire plant costing millions of pounds. In spite of the differences in scale, the principle of the separation is the same.

Figure 4.11 on page 50 shows you the way we can use a vapour pressure diagram to explain how distillation works. We heat a mixture of two liquids, A and B, with composition P. This begins to boil at temperature T_1. We now draw a line across the diagram until it hits the vapour line. The vapour has the composition Q. In a distillation experiment, the vapour given off from the boiling mixture is condensed, by using air or cold water to cool it. The vapour of composition Q will condense to a liquid of the *same* composition, Q. This liquid boils at temperature T_2. (Notice that this is a lower boiling point than that of the original mixture –

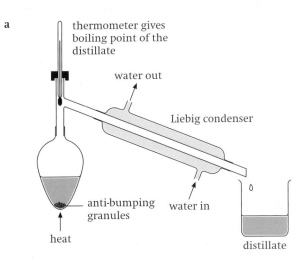

● **Figure 4.9** A typical laboratory simple distillation apparatus.

which it should be because the vapour contains a greater amount of the more volatile component.) When this liquid of composition Q boils, it gives off a vapour of composition R, which condenses to a liquid of even lower boiling point, T_3; and so on. Eventually, the vapour emerging from the distillation apparatus should be (almost) pure B.

In practice, 100% separation is impossible to achieve. One reason for this is that the liquid and vapour curves become closer and closer together. When they get very close, the difference between the liquid and its vapour is very, very little. If we wanted to separate them completely, we would need an infinite number of separation steps – and that is impossible.

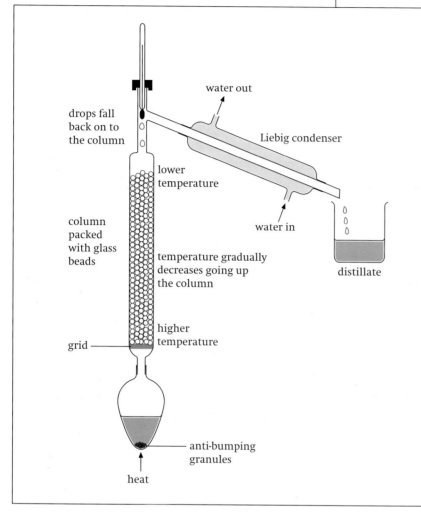

● **Figure 4.10** A fairly simple typical laboratory fractional distillation apparatus.

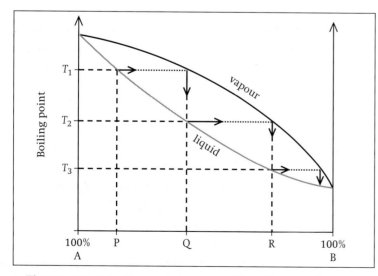

● **Figure 4.11** A boiling point–composition diagram for a mixture of two liquids, A and B. (See the text for an explanation of its use.)

More about simple and fractional distillation

■ *Simple distillation* is used to separate mixtures of miscible liquids that have widely differing boiling points (say 10 °C or more). If the liquids have very different boiling points, the vapour above the boiling mixture in the flask is likely to contain a significantly greater amount of the more volatile component. For example, simple distillation can be used to separate much of the ethanol from a mixture of ethanol and water. The boiling point of ethanol is 78 °C, which is over 20 °C less than that of water. If the mixture is distilled, almost pure ethanol reaches the thermometer bulb and, when this happens, the thermometer will read 78 °C. Indeed, the point of having the thermometer just at the outlet to the Liebig condenser is that, as soon as the reading starts to climb above 78 °C, it is a sure sign that the vapour no longer contains mainly ethanol, and water vapour is beginning to distil over. This is the time to stop the distillation.

Name of compound	Boiling point (°C)
1,2-Dimethylbenzene	145
1,3-Dimethylbenzene	139
Ethylbenzene	136

● **Table 4.3** Boiling points of three organic liquids.

■ *Fractional distillation* is used to separate mixtures of miscible liquids whose boiling points are similar, perhaps within a few degrees of each other. The idea is to have a gentle temperature gradient from the flask up to the outlet to the condenser, such that the temperature at the outlet is just at the temperature of the lowest boiling point liquid in the mixture.

For example, *table 4.3* gives the boiling points of three similar organic compounds. Suppose a mixture of the three were distilled. Let us assume that the mixture originally contained equal numbers of moles of each and boiled at 160 °C. Just above the boiling liquid in the flask, the vapour would contain *almost* identical quantities of the three compounds because they are so close in volatility. However, there would still be a little more ethylbenzene than 1,3-dimethylbenzene, with the highest boiling point component (1,2-dimethylbenzene) being the least abundant. This mixture of vapours would condense on the glass of the fractionating column, and on the glass beads. The liquid they make would have a lower boiling point than that of the liquid mixture in the flask (because it is richer in the more volatile components). However, this liquid will be heated by more of the vapour rising from the flask, and it will evaporate to give a vapour that is even richer in ethylbenzene (and in 1,3-dimethylbenzene). We shall guess that the temperature will be around 155 °C at this region of the column. A similar process as before takes place, with the vapour continually condensing and reboiling higher up the column; but with each layer higher on the column being at a slightly lower temperature than the layer below it. Provided the liquid in the flask is kept boiling gently, at each point on the column there will be an equilibrium (or nearly an equilibrium) between a liquid and its vapour, with a gradual decrease in temperature going up the

column. The aim would be to adjust the heating rate so that the temperature at the top of the column becomes just equal to 136 °C, the boiling point of the component with the lowest boiling point (ethylbenzene).

The efficiency of the separation relies on the efficiency of the exchange between liquid and vapour on the column. This is improved if there is a large area of contact between the liquid surface and the vapour. This is the reason why the fractionating column is usually packed with glass beads (although sometimes short pieces of glass tubing are used). The beads provide a huge surface area.

In practice it is sometimes necessary to lag the column, i.e. surround it with an insulating material. This is done if the liquid on the column loses heat too rapidly to the atmosphere, in which case the temperature at the top may never reach the boiling point of the lowest boiling point component.

Given that fractional distillation can be a slow process, it can be tempting to heat the flask strongly. However, if the flask is heated too quickly, there is insufficient time for equilibrium to be established further up the column. When this happens, you can get a short column of liquid travelling up the column. It is pushed up by the large amount of vapour being boiled off from below. This phenomenon is known as logging, and must be avoided if the distillation is to be a success.

SAQ 4.3

A student said that fractional distillation was rather like a very large number of simple distillations going on up the fractionating column. Do you agree?

SAQ 4.4

a Why is distillation using a Liebig condenser only likely to be a success when separating liquids with very different boiling points?

b In a distillation, we know that the vapour normally becomes richer in the more volatile component. What happens to the composition of the mixture remaining in the flask? Does its boiling point change or remain constant?

Industrial distillation

Two types of distillation column used in industry are shown in *figure 4.12*, and a schematic diagram of the operation of such columns is shown in *figure 4.13*. Industrial distillation is used for many purposes, one of the most important being the separation of different hydrocarbons from crude oil. The oil, known as the feedstock, is preheated and enters the distillation column about half-way

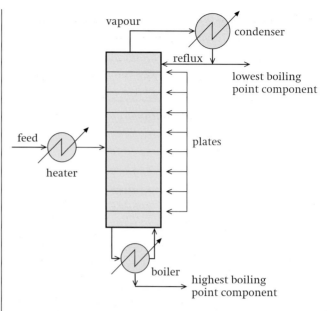

● **Figure 4.13** Diagram representing the operation of an industrial distillation column. In practice, some columns are designed to remove products at different heights up the column. The number of plates (or trays) needed varies depending on the mixture being separated.

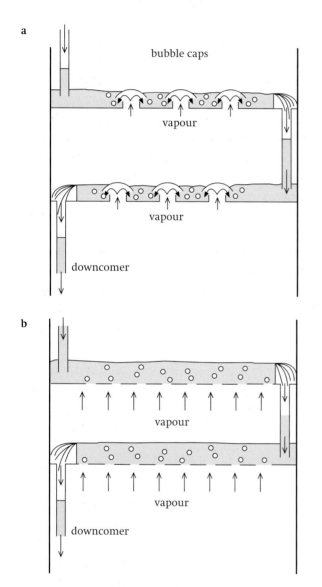

● **Figure 4.12** Two designs of industrial distillation column. In both approaches, the aim is to achieve a good equilibrium between the vapour and liquid phases.

a Hot vapours from below pass into the upper liquid layers by bubbling through holes in circular 'bubble caps'.

b Hot vapours rise up the column passing through a perforated metal plate into the liquid above.

up. There it meets a mixture of liquid and vapour that is already undergoing distillation. As we would expect, the more volatile components rise towards the top, and the less volatile components gravitate downwards. There is a heater at the bottom, which supplies energy to keep the distillation going. At various heights up the column there are metal plates perforated with holes. Liquid collects on the top of these plates and vapour from below bubbles up through the holes. In this way the liquid and vapour have the opportunity to reach equilibrium (although, in practice, they rarely do so). There are tubes at the side of the plates that allow liquid to flow back down the column. These tubes are the 'downcomers'. When liquid from a downcomer arrives at a lower plate, the higher temperature there brings about evaporation of the more volatile components, which then rise up through the perforated plates above. The less volatile components remain in the liquid and may run down another downcomer to the next plate below. A column like this will be left running indefinitely and a steady state is reached. At various heights up the column the various fractions are tapped off.

SAQ 4.5

Imagine that you have been given the task of designing an industrial distillation column that has to work continually (i.e. 24 hours per day every day of the year), and at a profit. Write down what you think are the main factors that have to be taken into account in completing your task.

Temperature (°C)	Mole fraction of benzene in liquid	Mole fraction of benzene in vapour
80.02	1	1
84	0.82	0.92
88	0.65	0.83
92	0.51	0.72
96	0.38	0.60
100	0.26	0.45
104	0.16	0.30
108	0.06	0.013
110.4	0	0

● **Table 4.4** Data for the boiling point–composition diagram of mixtures of benzene and methylbenzene.

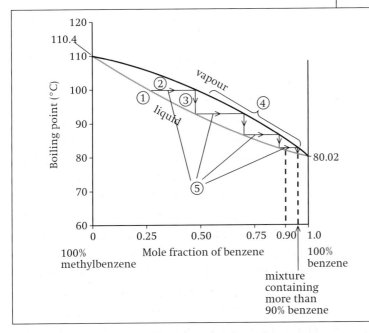

● **Figure 4.14** Boiling point–composition diagram for a mixture of benzene and methylbenzene. The circled numbers 1 to 5 represent the stages listed in the text. The number of theoretical plates needed to produce the desired mixture is obtained from the number of horizontal lines on the diagram.

Predicting the number of theoretical plates needed in a distillation

Look at the boiling point–composition diagram for a mixture of benzene and methylbenzene shown in *figure 4.14*. The diagram has been plotted using the data in *table 4.4*.

Suppose that we were given a mixture containing 25% of benzene, expressed as a proportion of the total number of moles of both liquids present. In other words, we have a mixture that has the mole fraction of benzene equal to 0.25. The question we are going to answer is this:

How many theoretical plates would be needed on a distillation column to produce a mixture with a mole fraction of benzene greater than 0.9 (or 90% benzene) starting from a mixture with a mole fraction of benzene equal to 0.25 (25% benzene)?

Here is the method (the stages correspond to the circled numbers on the diagram):

1 Find the point on the liquid composition line corresponding to the boiling point of the given mixture.

2 Draw the horizontal line that links the liquid to its vapour at its boiling point.

3 Now assume that you condense this vapour to give a liquid of the same composition, and draw the vertical line downwards to the liquid line on the diagram.

4 Repeat stages 2 and 3 until you find a vapour that condenses to a liquid that has a mole fraction of benzene greater than 0.9. This has been done for you on the diagram.

5 You then look at the diagram to see how many repeated vaporisations (followed by condensations) were needed. This is the number of horizontal lines on the diagram between 'liquid' and 'vapour', each of which represents a plate that would be needed on a real distillation column.

We now have the answer: *four* plates would be needed (assuming we count the plate on which the original liquid mixture started).

This method of calculating the number of plates is not very reliable because it disregards a great many factors that influence how a distillation proceeds in real life. For example, much depends on the quantities that are involved (which can be many tonnes per day), the rate at which heat can be supplied to the column, and the rate at which the distillate condenses as it is withdrawn from the column. In fact, in industrial processes, some of the final mixture that condenses is returned to the column. This practice is known as **reflux**. The rate at which reflux takes place can have a marked effect on the efficiency of the distillation.

There are other reasons why the course of distillations may not run as easily as one might want – as you will find in the next section.

SAQ 4.6

a Use the data in *table 4.5* to create the boiling point–composition diagram for a mixture of propanone and ethanol. [*Hint*: To prevent the vapour and liquid lines becoming too close together, use a fairly large scale for the boiling point axis, and start the scale at 50 °C (rather than going down to 0 °C).]

Temperature (°C)	Mole per cent propanone in vapour	Mole per cent propanone in liquid
56.1	100	100
57.0	92.9	90
58.0	86.5	80
59.1	80.2	70
60.4	73.9	60
61.8	67.4	50
63.6	60.5	40
65.9	52.4	30
69.0	41.7	20
73.0	26.2	10
78.3	0.0	0

● **Table 4.5** Composition data for a mixture of propanone and ethanol. (Data taken from *Chemical Engineering: A Special Study*, Longmans, 1985.)

b Predict how many plates would be needed to separate a mixture containing 10% mole fraction of propanone into a liquid with greater than 60% mole fraction of propanone.

c Why would it be difficult to separate the original mixture into one that contained greater than 90% mole fraction of propanone?

Does distillation always work?

The answer to this is 'no', it does not work if the mixture has a maximum or a minimum in its vapour pressure curve. To see why this is, we shall imagine carrying out a distillation of ethanol and water. This distillation is, of course, extremely important in the brewing industry. A mixture of ethanol and water shows a positive deviation from Raoult's law, and the vapour pressure curve has a maximum (like *figure 4.5b* on page 46). The boiling point–composition diagram for the mixture is shown in *figure 4.15*. Suppose that we started by distilling a mixture having 25% ethanol and 75% water with the intention of making 100% ethanol. If you follow the lines across the diagram, you can see that the vapour becomes increasingly richer in ethanol until the mixture of composition 95.6% ethanol plus 4.4% water is reached. This is the composition of the mixture that has the lowest boiling point (actually 78.2 °C). It is also the mixture that has the same composition for its vapour. Therefore, once this composition is reached on the distillation column, no more separation will take place. This mixture has a constant boiling point.

> A constant boiling point mixture is called an **azeotropic** mixture.

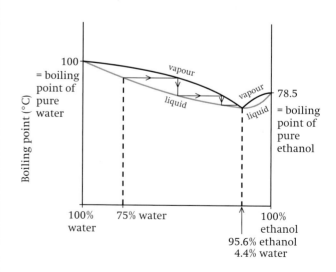

● **Figure 4.15** Boiling point–composition diagram for a mixture of ethanol and water. [*Note*: The composition scale has been exaggerated to make the diagram easier to read.]

In industry, azeotropic mixtures can sometimes be a nuisance, because you might think that the whole point of distilling a mixture is to be able to separate the components completely. One way of overcoming the problem is to add another liquid to a mixture. For example, if benzene is added to a mixture of ethanol and water, then an azeotropic mixture does not form. The ethanol that can be separated from the mixture is almost, but not completely, pure and certainly not safe enough to use in whisky, etc. Indeed, no one could drink more than a tiny quantity of completely pure alcohol and survive, and part of the pleasure that many people find in drinking different types of alcoholic drinks is that they have different tastes (because they contain more than just alcohol). So, brewers don't try to make completely pure alcohol.

SAQ 4.7

Figure 4.16 shows the boiling point–composition diagram for a solution of hydrochloric acid.

a What type of deviation from Raoult's law does the solution show?

b What would be produced if a solution of hydrochloric acid were distilled?

c What is the composition of the azeotropic mixture?

d What would be the result of distilling the mixture from **c**?

e Is it *always* true that the vapour above a mixture of two liquids that does not obey Raoult's law is richer in the more volatile liquid?

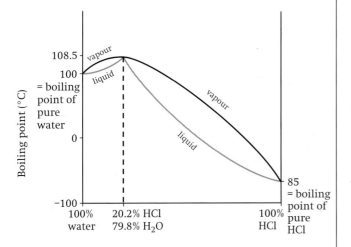

● **Figure 4.16** Boiling point–composition diagram for a mixture of hydrogen chloride and water, i.e. hydrochloric acid.

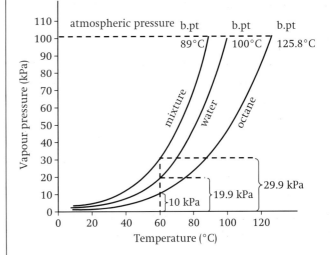

● **Figure 4.17** How the vapour pressures of water, octane and a mixture of the two change with temperature.

Steam distillation

If two immiscible liquids are kept stirred, the vapour pressure above the mixture is the total of the two separate vapour pressures. For example, octane and water are immiscible. At 25 °C, the vapour pressures of octane and water are approximately 3 kPa and 2.3 kPa. The vapour pressure above a mixture of them will be approximately 5.3 kPa. When the mixture is heated, the vapour pressure of both liquids will increase as shown in *figure 4.17*. The vapour pressure above the mixture is the sum of the individual vapour pressures. When the total pressure equals the atmospheric pressure, the mixture will boil. However, the diagram shows that this happens at nearly 89 °C, a temperature less than the boiling points of either the octane or the water. In other words, the introduction of steam has lowered the temperature at which the mixture will distil.

This is the reason why it can be useful to pass steam into a distillation mixture that contains an organic liquid (*figure 4.18* on page 56). For example, you may use steam distillation to separate the oil from orange peel, or perfumed oils from plants. Owing to the oil being organic, the steam is likely to be immiscible with it. The presence of the water in the mixture reduces its boiling point, and the organic liquid will distil at a lower

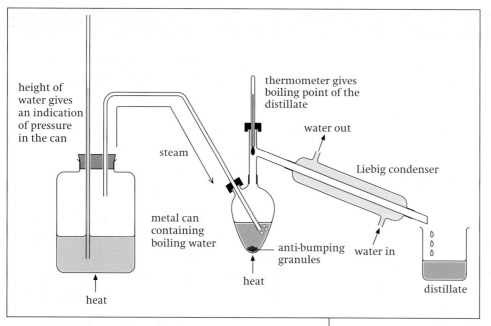

● **Figure 4.18** A typical laboratory steam distillation apparatus.

temperature. This is particularly useful if the organic substance is liable to decompose at temperatures near its normal boiling point. An added bonus is that the steam condensing in the organic mixture helps to heat it. However, the disadvantage is that the distillate will be a mixture of water and the organic liquid. Another method of separation has to be used to separate the organic substance. Sometimes it is possible to remove the water by adding a drying agent like anhydrous sodium sulphate. Alternatively, an organic solvent like ethoxyethane can be added. The organic substance will dissolve in the ethoxyethane, leaving the water behind. Finally the ethoxyethane can be distilled off very easily owing to its low boiling point. [*Safety note*: Ethoxyethane is highly volatile and flammable, so if you use this method, take care not to have naked flames in the vicinity.]

SAQ 4.8

Geraniums, roses, lavender and the leaves of many other plants contain a volatile and aromatic oil called *geraniol*. (They also contain many other compounds of course.) Suggest a way of isolating geraniol from the leaves of a plant.

SUMMARY

- A liquid boils when its vapour pressure equals the atmospheric pressure.

- The higher the vapour pressure of a liquid, the more volatile is the liquid.

- A liquid with a high vapour pressure will boil at a lower temperature than a liquid with a lower vapour pressure.

- Raoult's law says that: The vapour pressure of a solvent in a solution is equal to the vapour pressure of the pure solvent multiplied by its mole fraction in the solution. For example, in symbols: $p_A = N_A \times p_A^\circ$.

- Liquids that obey Raoult's law are called ideal liquids.

- Ideal liquids usually only have instantaneous dipole forces between their molecules. Non-ideal liquids often have hydrogen bonds between their molecules.

- Graphs of vapour pressure of a liquid mixture against composition:
  - are straight lines if the mixture obeys Raoult's law;
  - are curves if the mixture shows deviations from Raoult's law;
  - can show negative and positive deviations with, or without, a maximum or minimum.

- Whether a mixture is ideal or not depends on the attractions and repulsions between the different types of molecule.

- For a given mixture of liquids, graphs of boiling point against composition are curved in the opposite way to those of vapour pressure against composition.

- Boiling point–composition diagrams are used to explain how liquids are separated by distillation.

- The vapour above a mixture is richer in the more volatile component (the one with the higher vapour pressure and the liquid with the lower boiling point).

- Fractional distillation relies on achieving equilibrium between the vapour and liquid phases on the fractionating column. Equilibrium is favoured by having a large surface area of contact between the phases.

- A fractionating column can be split into a number of 'plates'. The number of theoretical plates required for separation of a mixture can be predicted from the boiling point–composition diagram.

- An azeotropic mixture has a constant boiling point and the composition of the vapour above the mixture is the same as that of the liquid. An azeotropic mixture cannot be separated by distillation.

- Steam distillation can be used to separate two immiscible liquids. It lowers the boiling point of the mixture, and this can reduce the chance of destroying heat-sensitive chemicals. Steam distillation is often used to separate an organic product from its mixture with water.

Questions

1   When glucose dissolves in water, the vapour pressure of water above the solution is less than that of pure water (at the same temperature). Glucose is a carbohydrate of formula $C_6H_{12}O_6$, and its molecule contains five OH groups. Suggest a reason why sugar dissolves in water, and why the vapour pressure of the solution is lowered compared to that of pure water.

2   In a mixture of trichloromethane and ethyl ethanoate, there are strong intermolecular forces between the two types of molecule. Would you expect the mixture to give a positive or a negative deviation from Raoult's law?

3   Petrol and water are immiscible. You may assume that petrol is made of the hydrocarbon octane, C_8H_{18}.
    a   What type of bonding holds octane molecules together?
    b   What type of intermolecular bonding holds water molecules together?
    c   Compare the strengths of the bonds between two octane molecules, between two water molecules, and between a water molecule and an octane molecule.
    d   Explain why octane and water are immiscible.

4   The vapour pressure of ethoxyethane is 57.855 kPa and that of propanone is 23.541 kPa at 25 °C. Which one boils at 34.7 °C and which at 56.4 °C?

5   A laboratory fractional distillation column is often filled with glass beads.
    a   Why is the column not left empty?
    b   Suggest a reason why it is better to use a large number of small glass beads than, say, a small number of large glass marbles in a laboratory distillation column?
    c   Why are industrial distillation columns not packed with glass beads?

6   A mixture of carbon disulphide and propanone shows a positive deviation from Raoult's law. Their vapour pressures are (approximately) 39 kPa and 24 kPa at 25 °C.
    a   If a mixture of 0.2 mol carbon disulphide and 0.8 mol propanone were made, what would be the vapour pressure of the mixture if it were ideal?
    b   How would the true vapour pressure of the mixture compare with the ideal value?
    c   One of the pair of liquids has a boiling point of 46 °C, and the other 56 °C. Which liquid has which boiling point?

7   Use the graph that you drew in SAQ 4.6a to answer the following:
    a   Remind yourself of the formulae of propanone and ethanol, and then work out the mole fraction of propanone in a mixture that contains 29 g propanone and 34.5 g ethanol.
    b   What would be the normal boiling point of this mixture?
    c   If the vapour of this mixture were condensed, what would be the mole fraction of propanone in the resulting liquid?

Answers to questions

Chapter 1

Answers to self-assessment questions

1.1 There is no hydrogen bonding in methane.

1.2
  a Temperature increasing is another way of saying that the average energy of the particles is increasing. Thus, the number of particles with high energies increases, and their kinetic energy can overcome the intermolecular forces that hold the particles together. When this happens, the particles with higher-than-average energy can escape from the liquid into the gas.
  b With very few exceptions, every substance has its own particular boiling point because it is made of a unique set of molecules that have their own unique set of intermolecular forces, and therefore a unique temperature at which these forces can be overcome.

1.3 The molecules most likely to leave the surface at first are the most energetic. Thus, if ethanol or propanone loses some of its most energetic molecules, the average energy of the remainder goes down. Therefore, the temperature of the liquid goes down. As the temperature of the liquid goes down, the heat from your hand gives energy to those molecules that are left. This results in your hand cooling.

1.4 Water vapour escapes from the Earth's surface (damp ground, lakes, seas, etc.), rises in the atmosphere, and as it does so it cools. When a region of the atmosphere becomes saturated with water vapour, tiny water droplets start to form. Clouds are large collections of these tiny droplets. A number of things can happen to a cloud. If the surrounding atmosphere is not saturated with water vapour, the droplets will lose more molecules to the surroundings by evaporation than they gain; in this situation the cloud disperses. If a state of equilibrium is reached with the surroundings, then the cloud will just go on existing. If there is slight imbalance with the surroundings, the cloud may (i) gradually get smaller as the water droplets slowly evaporate, or (ii) get bigger as more water droplets form because the surrounding atmosphere becomes saturated with water vapour. In the latter case, eventually the droplets themselves will coalesce and be too heavy to be supported in the atmosphere: the result is rain.

1.5
  a The average energy increases.
  b Note that not every molecule is bound to suffer an increase; some may travel more slowly than before owing to the way they collide with other molecules; but the overall effect is for the majority of molecules to increase their energies.

1.6 Because the pressure is the same (atmospheric pressure), the reason why the volumes are different is that the cylinders are in rooms kept at different temperatures. Cylinder B is in the room with the higher temperature (the volume is the larger of the two).

1.7 We have $P = 100\,\text{kPa} = 100 \times 10^3\,\text{Pa}$, $V = 1\,\text{dm}^3$ $= 1 \times 10^{-3}\,\text{m}^3$ and $T = 20\,°\text{C} = (20 + 273)\,\text{K} = 293\,\text{K}$, so that $n = \dfrac{PV}{RT} = \dfrac{100 \times 10^3\,\text{Pa} \times 10^{-3}\,\text{m}^3}{8.314\,\text{J}\,\text{K}^{-1}\,\text{mol}^{-1} \times 293\,\text{K}} = 0.041\,\text{mol}$.

1.8 As the balloon rises, the pressure of the atmosphere decreases, thus the gas inside will expand and the envelope expands. If the envelope were full at the start, it would be likely to burst at high altitude. High-altitude balloons are often coated with a bright silver-coloured coating. This helps to reflect the Sun's rays and keep the balloon cool, thus preventing even more expansion taking place. (The silver layer can also help the balloon to show up on radar.)

1.9
  a Volume occupied $= 64 \times 10^{-30}\,\text{m}^3 \times$ $6.02 \times 10^{23}\,\text{mol}^{-1} = 3.85 \times 10^{-5}\,\text{m}^3 = 38.5\,\text{cm}^3$
  b This is about 0.2% of the total volume.

1.10 At low pressure the particles are very far apart, so the influence of intermolecular forces is very slight. Also, the proportion of the total volume that the molecules occupy becomes extremely small; i.e. the molecules can be assumed to be like points. These are the assumptions made about ideal gases.

1.11 At room temperature and pressure, 1 mol occupies about 24 dm³. Thus the answers are:

a 48 dm³

b 6 dm³

1.12 **a** The liquid can evaporate from the tip of the small syringe. Therefore less liquid is injected than was weighed out.

b It increases the value of the relative molecular mass. To see why, let us take an impossible example, but one that illustrates the working. Suppose the syringe and liquid start out with a mass of 3 g, and that after injection their mass is 1 g. We believe that 2 g of liquid has been injected. However, let us assume that 1 g of liquid actually evaporated before the injection took place. Therefore the actual mass injected was only 1 g. If the gas occupied 100 cm³ at room temperature and pressure, we would calculate the relative molecular mass to be 2 g mol⁻¹ × 24 000 cm³/100 cm³ = 480 g mol⁻¹ (We have already said that the numbers are not very likely!) Its true value should be 1 g mol⁻¹ × 24 000 cm³/100 cm³ = 240 g mol⁻¹ i.e. half the experimental result.

1.13 You should find that M(propanone) = 58.6 g mol⁻¹. Propanone has the formula $(CH_3)_2CO$, and a relative molecular mass of about 58 g mol⁻¹, so the result is reasonable.

Answers to end-of-chapter questions

1 **a** Diamond is made of a giant structure of interconnecting tetrahedra of carbon atoms. In effect, every carbon atom is connected to every other, thus giving a lattice of immense strength. You should have met this structure in other parts of your course.

b Nitrogen is a fairly electronegative element, thus making the N–H bonds polar. The ammonia molecule is tetrahedral. The single lone pair of electrons on the nitrogen acts as a density of negative charge that can hydrogen bond with a hydrogen atom on a neighbouring molecule.

c Instantaneous dipole forces between the molecules. Although there are many hydrogen atoms, carbon atoms are insufficiently electronegative to make the C–H bonds polar. Thus hydrogen bonding cannot occur.

d The structure of an alcohol molecule is similar to that of a water molecule. Although there is only one O–H bond in an alcohol, the bond is polar, and hydrogen bonding is possible. It is the possibility of hydrogen bonding in ethanol that allows it to mix with water in beers and other alcoholic drinks.

e The alkanes have lower boiling points because the instantaneous dipole forces are weaker than the hydrogen bonds in the alcohols.

2 See *figure*.

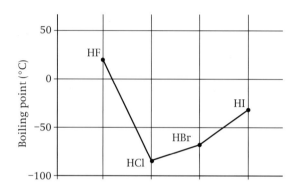

● **Answer for** end-of-chapter question 2

Hydrogen fluoride has the lowest molecular mass, and we might expect it to have the lowest boiling point of the four hydrides; but it has the highest boiling point. The cause is very strong hydrogen bonding between the molecules in HF. HCl, HBr and HI have only dipole–dipole forces. Their boiling points increase with molecular mass, as we might expect.

3 It is a common misconception that the bubbles in boiling water are made of air (or oxygen). Rather, the bubbles are bubbles of steam, i.e. water vapour at 100 °C (assuming normal atmospheric pressure). At this temperature, water molecules have enough energy to overcome the hydrogen bonds between them and they fly apart, forming a pocket of gas. If enough molecules do this, we see bubbles appearing.

4 As you go up a mountain, the atmospheric pressure decreases. Therefore, it becomes easier for the vapour pressure of water to equal the atmospheric pressure, and so the temperature at which water boils will decrease. Mountaineers have to contend with this because, even though a pot of water may be boiling, its temperature may be only 60 °C (say) rather than 100 °C. Therefore cooking times increase.

5　**a** There is nothing between them, i.e. empty space. If you have said there is a 'vacuum' then you are correct, provided that you realise that a vacuum is just another name for empty space.

b 2.5×10^7

c Well, no!

d You would see a gap about 1.25×10^7 m in front of you (if only you could see that far); i.e. about 4 times the diameter of the Earth. The point of this is to persuade you that, as far as a gas molecule is concerned, even the smallest diameter tube that might be attached to the vacuum pump is of an enormous size.

e See *figure*. Your diagram should look like the one shown below – the only difference from the diagram given in the question is that there are fewer molecules in the container.

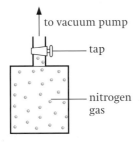

● **Answer for** end-of-chapter question 5e

f If you have drawn a diagram with some other arrangement, then you probably have not realised that a vacuum pump is a device for reducing the pressure of a gas to a very low value. (A perfect vacuum is impossible to achieve – there will always be some molecules left.) When the tap is opened, some molecules inside the container will find their way out by chance – the vacuum pump does *not* 'suck' them out. Remember the scale of the space open to the gas molecules when going down the connecting tube: there is so much space and very little in their way to stop them moving down the tube when they happen to be moving that way.

6　Trichloromethane is a highly polar molecule, and so dipole–dipole bonding can take place between its molecules. Therefore it shows large deviations from ideal gas behaviour, and the ideal gas equation cannot be expected to give good results. The outcome will be an abnormal relative molecular mass.

Chapter 2

Answers to self-assessment questions

2.1　**a** See *figure*. The temperature at which solid carbon dioxide and the gas can be in equilibrium is 200 K (at 100 kPa).

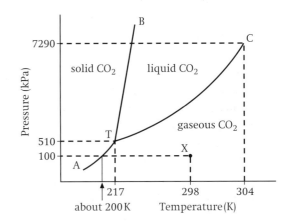

● **Answer for** SAQ 2.1a

b At 100 kPa presure no temperature exists at which liquid carbon dioxide can occur. Dry ice changes directly into gaseous carbon dioxide as the temperature increases from 200 K to 298 K.

c No.

2.2　**a** 273.16 K and 0.6 kPa.

b This point is on the vapour pressure curve, and there will be an equilibrium between the liquid and vapour phases.

c Above the critical point temperature, 647.4 K.

d No. Ice will only sublime at conditions along the sublimation curve (AT in *figures 2.6* and *2.7*), for which the pressure has to be below 0.6 kPa.

2.3　**a** Melting points vary with pressure so, strictly, all melting points should be quoted at a specific pressure. However, generally we assume that the pressure is 100 kPa unless it is stated otherwise.

b Solid and liquid.

c An accurate melting point will only be obtained if the system is at (or at least very close to) equilibrium. If the sample were cooled quickly, the system would not be able to come to equilibrium, so the measured melting point would be in error.

2.4 **a** See *figure*.

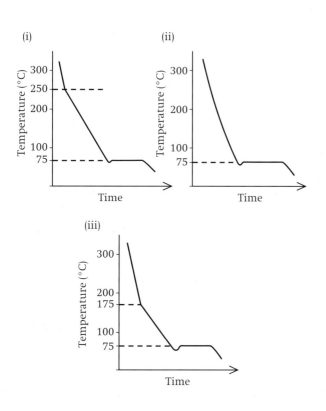

● **Answer for** SAQ 2.4a

b (i) P consists only of a liquid containing a mixture of X and Y. (ii) Q consists of a liquid mixture of X and Y together with solid Y. (iii) R contains a liquid mixture of X and Y together with solid X. (iv) S consists of solid Y and eutectic. (v) T contains solid X and eutectic.

c Point M corresponds to a liquid mixture containing about 60% X and 40% Y. When the liquid cools, the composition stays the same but the temperature drops. If you draw a line vertically downwards from M, it meets the equilibrium line at about 150 °C. This is the temperature at which solid X starts to crystallise. As the mixture cools, more X comes out of the liquid. This leaves the mixture richer in Y, and eventually the liquid remaining will contain 40% X and 60% Y – the eutectic composition. When this happens, the whole of the remaining liquid starts to crystallise, giving a final solid containing particles of X and solid eutectic.

2.5 Yes, the lattice is disrupted, so that the planes of metal atoms do not line up as perfectly as in the pure metal. Again, this prevents the layers separating as abruptly as in the pure metal.

2.6 Applying Le Chatelier's principle in this case means that supplying heat to a system in equilibrium (i.e. increasing the temperature) should cause the equilibrium to shift in the direction that removes heat, i.e. tends to lower the temperature, by absorbing heat energy. Therefore, an equilibrium mixture should move in the direction of the endothermic change. So salts that dissolve endothermically in water should have solubilities that increase with temperature. [*Word of warning*: In practice, dissolving is rarely done under equilibrium conditions; but the prediction still works.]

2.7 Before modern (mechanical) fridges and freezers were invented, a freezing mixture of ice and salt was often used to cool other mixtures to below their freezing points (e.g. ice cream) and to keep substances cold (as if they were in a fridge).

Answers to end-of-chapter questions

1 In *figure 2.3*, you can see that, as the pressure increases, the temperature at which solid carbon dioxide can be in equilibrium with its liquid phase also increases (i.e. the melting point curve BT slopes to the right). Thus, as the pressure increases, the melting point rises.

2 At the triple point, 510 kPa and 217 K.

3 **a** Moving up the phase diagram at 217 K brings us into the 'solid CO_2' region, so only the solid phase would exist at equilibrium.
b The point corresponding to this pair of values lies in the 'liquid CO_2' region, so only the liquid phase would exist at equilibrium.

4 At the triple point: 273.16 K and 0.6 kPa.

5 When the pressure of the water vapour became equal to that of the atmosphere, the water would boil. From the phase diagram in *figure 2.6*, we can see that boiling would occur at 3 kPa. By the way, be careful to distinguish the way that the word 'pressure' is used. For example, when we draw the vapour pressure curve on a phase diagram, the pressure plotted is the pressure of the water vapour at equilibrium, not that of the surrounding atmosphere. If the water is trapped in a flask, and the pressure inside the flask is reduced to 3 kPa, then as far as the water is concerned 3 kPa becomes the atmospheric pressure.

6 The cause is hydrogen bonding.

7 For carbon dioxide, and many other substances, the solid phase is more tightly packed than the liquid phase. For water, the reverse is true: ice is less densely packed than liquid water at the melting point. Increasing the pressure tends to keep molecules in a solid even more tightly packed. For carbon dioxide, this makes it even harder to move the molecules apart from one another, so more heat energy is needed to melt the solid. For ice, increasing the pressure favours the liquid phase, because there the molecules can squeeze together more tightly; hence the melting point decreases.

8 Again, the reason is hydrogen bonding in water. Carbon dioxide is not a polar molecule, and its instantaneous dipole forces are relatively weak.

9 **a** See *figure.*

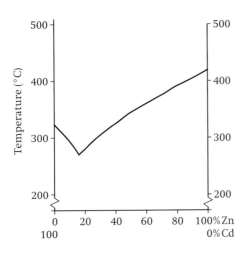

● **Answer for** end-of-chapter question 9a

b See *figure.* [*Note*: Depending on the accuracy of your graph, you may find the changes in the slope of the graph to be at slightly different temperatures.]

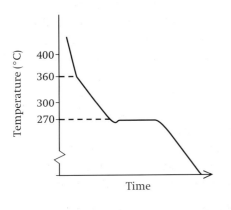

● **Answer for** end-of-chapter question 9b

c The solid would contain solid zinc, and eutectic containing 17% zinc.

10 Strictly, we cannot predict with certainty anything about how *fast* a process takes place from the data. Even if we know that a salt dissolves to a great extent, this does not *necessarily* mean it will dissolve quickly – but usually it does. The point is that the solubility data are obtained at equilibrium, and we have no way of knowing how long it takes for equilibrium to be achieved. An excellent example of this is the fact that the equilibrium for the reaction between diamond and oxygen lies in favour of the product of the reaction, carbon dioxide. However, no one has yet seen the reaction take place under normal atmospheric conditions: the reaction is almost infinitely slow. Hence, diamonds retain their value.

11 You would have to take account of the following points:
   (i) 100 g of water would have to be weighed out accurately into a flask.
   (ii) To keep the flask at a constant temperature, it would have to be placed in a thermostatted bath of water.
   (iii) Salt would be added to the solution until no more would dissolve; i.e. some salt should be left in the flask in contact with the solution.
   (iv) The solution should be left for at least ten minutes to come to equilibrium.
   (v) A measured volume of the solution should be withdrawn from the flask, e.g. using a pipette, but making sure that no solid was removed with the solution.
   (vi) The sample should be analysed. There are two ways of doing this: either you could perform a silver nitrate titration to discover the number of moles of chloride ion present (and hence the number of moles, and mass, of sodium chloride); or you could carefully evaporate the solution and weigh the sodium chloride left.
   (vii) Finally you would scale up the result of your analysis to give the mass of salt in the original 100 g of water.

Chapter 3

Answers to self-assessment questions

3.1 **a** Using Henry's law and the value from *table 3.2* for CO_2, you get

$[CO_2(aq)]/p_{CO_2} = 3.37 \times 10^{-4} \, mol \, dm^{-3} \, kPa^{-1}$

Rearranging and substituting $p_{CO_2} = 1000 \, kPa$ gives the concentration of dissolved CO_2 gas as

$[CO_2(aq)] = 3.37 \times 10^{-4} \, mol \, dm^{-3} \, kPa^{-1} \times 10^3 \, kPa$

$= 0.337 \, mol \, dm^{-3}$

So the mass of gas dissolved

$= 0.337 \, mol \, dm^{-3} \times 44 \, g \, mol^{-1} = 14.83 \, g \, dm^{-3}$

Finally, 1 litre = 1 dm^3, so 14.83 g of CO_2 would be dissolved in a 1 litre bottle.

b Bubbles of carbon dioxide rapidly escape from the liquid (hence the 'fizz') because the pressure is released and the system is no longer at equilibrium.

c When the pressure of the gas is reduced to 100 kPa, 3.37×10^{-2} mol of gas would dissolve in 1 dm^3, i.e. 1.48 g in 1 litre. Thus, in the 750 cm^3 remaining, there would be

$1.48 \, g \times 750 \, cm^3/100 \, cm^3 = 1.11$ g of carbon dioxide dissolved.

d The volumes are:

$24 \, dm^3 \, mol^{-1} \times 0.337 \, mol = 8.09 \, dm^3$ and

$24 \, dm^3 \, mol^{-1} \times 1.11 \, g/44 \, g \, mol^{-1} = 0.61 \, dm^3$

e We can estimate that almost the entire amount of carbon dioxide will escape into the atmosphere. So, the estimated mass is $14.8 \, g \times 20 \times 20 \times 52 = 307 \, 840$ g, which is over 300 kg. This may give you some idea of the huge amounts of carbon dioxide that are released into the atmosphere by way of the soft drinks industry.

3.2 The structure of the ethanol molecule is similar to that of water (see *figure*). Both molecules contain hydrogen atoms directly bonded to a highly electronegative oxygen atom. These hydrogen atoms carry a partial positive charge and are available for hydrogen bonding to an oxygen atom on a neighbouring molecule. Thus the structures of water and ethanol molecules allow hydrogen bonding not only between water molecules and between ethanol molecules, *but also* between water and ethanol molecules in a mixture of the two liquids. Note that the hydrogen atoms bonded to carbon are not involved in hydrogen bonding because the carbon–hydrogen bond is not sufficiently polar.

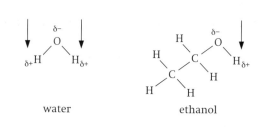

water   ethanol

● **Answer for** SAQ 3.2

3.3 **a** False. Sodium chloride is ionic and will not dissolve in a purely covalent, non-polar liquid. (There are no attractions between the liquid and ions that can overcome the attractive forces holding the ions in the crystal lattice.)

b True (both covalent).

c True (both covalent).

d True (both can hydrogen bond).

e False (probably). You were expected to predict that the polar nature of the OH bond in the butan-1-ol would lessen the chances of complete miscibility with a purely covalent liquid.

3.4 **a** After the first extraction, there was 0.0230 g of iodine left in 40 cm^3 of the aqueous layer. Again, let us say that x grams of this iodine goes into 20 cm^3 of the organic layer at equilibrium. Then,

concentration of iodine in tetrachloromethane

$= x/20 \, g \, cm^{-3}$

concentration of iodine in aqueous layer

$= (0.0230 - x)/40 \, g \, cm^{-3}$

Therefore

$$\frac{x/20}{(0.0230 - x)/40} = 85$$

which gives

$2x = 85 \times (0.0230 - x)$

$2x = 85 \times 0.0230 - 85x$

$87x = 85 \times 0.0230$

$x = 85 \times 0.0230/87$

and thus

$x = 0.0225$

The result is that only 0.0230 g − 0.0225 g = 0.0005 g of iodine would be left in the aqueous layer.

b In this case,

concentration of iodine in tetrachloromethane

$= x/40\,g\,cm^{-3}$

concentration of iodine in aqueous layer

$= (1 - x)/40\,g\,cm^{-3}$

Therefore

$$\frac{x/40}{(1 - x)/40} = 85$$

which gives

$x = 85(1 - x)$

$x = 85 - 85x$

and thus

$x = 85/86 = 0.9884$

So 0.9884 g are extracted into the organic layer, and there would be 1.0000 g − 0.9884 g = 0.0116 g of iodine left in the aqueous layer. This is a better result than one extraction with 20 cm³, but not so good as two repeated extractions with 20 cm³.

c In general, two repeated extractions are better than one (using same total volume of solvent).

3.5 a The number of moles of iodine in the aqueous layer before adding the organic liquid is $0.1 \times 50\,cm^3/1000\,cm^3 = 0.005\,mol$. If we assume that x mol of iodine goes into the organic layer at equilibrium, we have

concentration of iodine in organic layer

$= x/10\,mol\,cm^{-3}$

concentration of iodine in aqueous layer

$= (0.005 - x)/50\,mol\,cm^{-3}$

Therefore,

$$\frac{x/10}{(0.005 - x)/50} = 100$$

$$x/10 = 100 \times (0.005 - x)/50$$

$$x = 20 \times (0.005 - x)$$

$$x = 0.1/21 = 0.004\,76$$

There were 0.004 76 mol of iodine in the organic layer at equilibrium. This number of moles was in 10 cm³, so the number of moles in 1000 cm³ would be 0.004 76 mol × 1000 cm³/10 cm³ = 0.476 mol. The concentration is written as 0.476 mol dm⁻³.

b Mass of iodine present = 0.004 76 mol × 254 g mol⁻¹ = 1.210 g.

c The original mass of iodine present was 0.005 mol × 254 g mol⁻¹ = 1.27 g, so the mass remaining would be 0.060 g.

Answers to end-of-chapter questions

1 The product is sulphuric acid. However, the reaction can be explosively violent. In industry, sulphur trioxide is dissolved in previously made concentrated sulphuric acid. This is a much less violent reaction, and then the product is diluted with water to make the sulphuric acid that is used in laboratories.

2 **a** Hydrogen bonding occurs in both substances.
   b Because hydrogen bonds can occur between water molecules, and between ammonia molecules, we expect hydrogen bonds to occur between water and ammonia molecules. Hence it is easy for ammonia to mix with water.

3 The graph of solubility against pressure is very nearly a straight line. The slope gives the value of Henry's constant. You should find a value around $3.4 \times 10^{-4}\,mol\,dm^{-3}\,kPa^{-1}$.

4 **a** The key to this question is to realise that, if the bottle is left open for a long time, there will be an equilibrium set up between the carbon dioxide in the water and that in the atmosphere. The Henry's law constant for carbon dioxide tells us that $3.37 \times 10^{-4}\,mol$ of the gas would dissolve in 1 dm³ of water at 25 °C if the pressure of the gas were 100 kPa. However, the pressure of the gas is only 0.03 kPa. Hence the concentration would only be

$0.03\,kPa \times 3.37 \times 10^{-4}\,mol\,dm^{-3}\,kPa^{-1}$

$= 1.01 \times 10^{-5}\,mol\,dm^{-3}$.

That is, $1.01 \times 10^{-5}\,mol$ of gas would *remain* in the water.

b Using the ideal gas equation in the form $V = nRT/P$, we have

$$V = \frac{1.01 \times 10^{-5}\,mol \times 8.314\,J\,K^{-1}\,mol^{-1} \times 298\,K}{3 \times 10^3\,Pa}$$

$= 8.35 \times 10^{-6}\,m^3$

$= 8.35\,cm^3$

5 The solution has to be left to come to equilibrium before we can apply Henry's law.

6 Ionic substances are solids at room temperature and pressure, so cannot dissolve other substances. However, if the temperature is raised above their melting points, then their properties as liquids *can* be investigated.

7 Initially, the aqueous layer is dark brown and the organic layer is clear. When the mixture is shaken, some of the iodine molecules dissolve in the organic liquid. This removes iodine from the left-hand side of the equation. According to Le Chatelier's principle, the equilibrium in the aqueous layer will shift in the direction that tends to replace these molecules. That is, the equilibrium shown in the equation shifts to the left. Thus the concentration of I_3^- ions reduces. Thus we would see the organic layer becoming tinged with purple, and the intensity of the brown colour in the aqueous layer decrease. As time goes on, the effect becomes more pronounced. Eventually, equilibrium is achieved between the iodine molecules dissolved in the organic layer and those in the aqueous layer. This is the equilibrium to which the partition law applies. When equilibrium between the two layers is reached, the organic layer becomes quite strongly coloured purple. However, the aqueous layer will remain a light brown colour – some of the iodine will always remain in the aqueous layer trapped as I_3^- ions.

8   In theory it is impossible to remove 100% of the iodine because there would always be some left in the aqueous layer at equilibrium. So, strictly, the answer is an infinite number. However, you have seen in the calculations that, even after just two extractions, the amount of iodine left can become very small. For most practical purposes, there would be little point doing more than three or four extractions.

9   a Concentration of dichloromethane in the octan-1-ol is $33\,g\,dm^{-3}$.
     b Concentration of dichloromethane in the water layer is $1.84\,g\,dm^{-3}$.
     c $K_{pc} = 17.9$
     d It evaporates into the air, which is a potential health hazard.

Chapter 4

Answers to self-assessment questions

4.1   a $n_{hexane} = 17.2\,g/86\,g\,mol^{-1} = 0.2\,mol$ and $n_{heptane} = 30\,g/100\,g\,mol^{-1} = 0.3\,mol$. Thus, $N_{hexane} = 0.2/0.5 = 0.4$, and $N_{heptane} = 0.6$.
      b $p_{hexane} = 0.4 \times p_A^\circ = 0.4 \times 16.1\,kPa = 6.44\,kPa$ and $p_{heptane} = 2.82\,kPa$.
      c $9.26\,kPa$.
      d Hexane.
      e Hexane – it has the higher vapour pressure.

4.2   a Hexane and pentane are both alkanes, so are expected to make an ideal mixture.

b Propan-1-ol and water can hydrogen bond together, so we would expect them to show a negative deviation from Raoult's law.

4.3   The student was right – the greater the number of 'mini-distillations' on the column, the better.

4.4   a If the liquids have very close boiling points, then the vapours of both are bound to find their way into the condenser and it will be impossible to separate them. If one liquid has a much lower boiling point than the other, its vapour will go into the condenser much more easily than the other.
      b The mixture in the flask becomes richer in the less volatile component. Its B. pt increases.

4.5   You would have to take into account the balance between achieving a high degree of separation against the rate at which the separation could be achieved, and the cost of building and maintaining the plant. For example, for excellent separation, a long column with a large number of plates is good, but the distillation would take longer. This would lower the yield each day, and therefore lower the potential profit. The physical size of a column can make a great difference to the cost of its manufacture – the more steel, the greater the cost. You would also have to take into account the energy changes in the process. Heat is need to keep the column going, both to provide thermal energy and to keep the various pumps and heat exchangers working. In short, the design of a chemical process on an industrial scale is a complicated task.

4.6   a See *figure*.

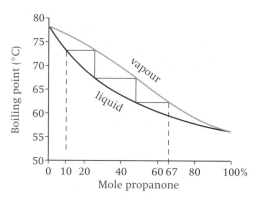

● **Answer for** SAQ 4.6a

      b By drawing the horizontal and vertical lines shown in the figure, you should find that it requires three plates (in theory).

c As the proportion of propanone increases, the liquid and vapour lines get closer together. This means that there is an increasingly small difference between their compositions. In turn, this would make it difficult to separate the liquid and vapour because such a small difference in temperature would be needed between the plates.

4.7 **a** The solution shows a *negative* deviation from Raoult's law, with a minimum in the vapour pressure curve. (Remember that the boiling point shows a maximum when there is a minimum in the vapour pressure curve, and vice versa. Raoult's law refers to the vapour pressure curve.)

b In theory, water would be the final distillate. (But in practice, because hydrogen chloride is so volatile, it would be extremely difficult to get pure water.)

c The azeotropic mixture contains 20.2% HCl and 79.8% H_2O.

d The liquid in the flask would finally become the azeotropic mixture and it would distil to give a vapour (and distillate) of the same composition.

e No, it is not always true. Azeotropic mixtures are exceptions.

4.8 The basic recipe is to cut the aromatic parts of the plant (often this is the leaves) into small portions, and subject them to steam distillation. For your information, the structure of geraniol is $(CH_3)_2$=CHCH$_2$CH$_2$C(CH$_3$)=CHCH$_2$OH

Answers to end-of-chapter questions

1 Because of the OH groups, there are many opportunities for water molecules to hydrogen bond to a glucose molecule. Therefore, the attractive forces between the water and glucose molecules can overcome the (mainly) instantaneous dipole forces holding glucose molecules in the crystal. The attractions between glucose and water molecules help to prevent water molecules escaping so easily into the vapour.

2 Negative deviation.

3 **a** Instantaneous dipole bonding.
b Hydrogen bonding.
c The strengths would vary in the order water−water > octane−octane > water−octane.
d It is energetically unfavourable to replace strong hydrogen bonds in water with much weaker bonds between unlike molecules.

4 Ethoxyethane has the higher vapour pressure, so it has the lower boiling point (34.7 °C).

5 **a** Separation of the components in a mixture depends upon an equilibrium being set up between the liquid and its vapour at each temperature. If there is no surface for the vapour to condense on, there will be no liquid surface, and no equilibrium – and hence no reliable separation. An exception will be on the surface of the column, but this is a relatively small surface when you consider the total volume of space available to the vapour.

b A large number of small balls has a greater surface area than a small number of large balls.

c There are many reasons, for example: the weight of the beads in a column 30 m high and 2 m diameter would be enormous; getting the vapour and liquid to move up a column packed in this way would be difficult; maintenance would be a problem; glass fractures easily.

6 **a** The mole fractions of carbon disulphide and propanone are 0.2 and 0.8, respectively. (Note that these are the same as the number of moles of each *only* because the numbers of moles add up to 1.0 in total – in general the number of moles of each liquid and their mole fractions are *not* the same values.) Thus, assuming Raoult's law is obeyed:
$p_{carbon\ disulphide}$ = 7.8 kPa and $p_{propanone}$ = 19.2 kPa. Thus the total vapour pressure would be 27 kPa.

b The true vapour pressure of the mixture would be greater than 27 kPa.

c Carbon disulphide has the greater vapour pressure, so it has the lower boiling point.

7 **a** The formulae of propanone and ethanol are $(CH_3)_2CO$ and C_2H_5OH, respectively. Their molar masses are 58 g mol^{-1} and 46 g mol^{-1}, respectively. Thus the quantities involved are 29 g/(58 g mol^{-1}) = 0.5 mol and 34.5 g/(46 g mol^{-1}) = 0.75 mol, which gives a total of 1.25 mol. The mole fraction of propanone in the mixture is 0.5/1.25 = 0.4, or 40%.

b From the graph given in the answer for SAQ 4.6a, the boiling point is about 64 °C.

c Drawing a horizontal line from the liquid to vapour line and then dropping a vertical line onto the composition axis should give you a mole fraction for propanone of about 61%.

Glossary

absolute scale see *Kelvin scale*.

alloy a mixture containing a metal and one or more other metals (or non- metals).

azeotropic mixture a mixture that has a constant boiling point. Such a mixture cannot be separated by (simple) distillation.

boiling point the temperature at which the vapour pressure of a liquid becomes equal to the atmospheric pressure—normally taken as 100 kPa. Also, the temperature at which (for a given pressure) the liquid and gaseous forms of a substance can exist in equilibrium.

boiling point diagram a graph of boiling point against composition for liquid mixtures. The diagram allows the course of a distillation to be predicted.

Brownian motion the name given to the random movement of molecules.

critical point at temperatures above the critical point a gas cannot be turned into a liquid.

deviations from Raoult's law solutions that don't obey Raoult's law are said to show deviations from his law.

distillation the process of separating the components of a liquid mixture by heating them and driving off the lower boiling point component(s).

elastic collisions collisions between molecules where there is no overall change in their total kinetic energy. See *ideal gas*.

electron cloud the volume around the nucleus of an atom where the electrons spend most of their time.

equilibrium a condition where there is no overall change in the proportions of the reactants and products in a chemical change, even though the reactions are still going on. At equilibrium the rate of the forward reaction equals the rate of the backward reaction.

eutectic the solid that separates from a mixture of two substances that has the lowest melting point of all possible mixtures of the two substances. The eutectic mixture has a melting point curve like that of a pure substance. Also, see Box 2A on page 25.

eutectic temperature the temperature at which a eutectic mixture separates from a mixture.

fractional distillation A multi-stage distillation used to separate a mixture of three or more liquids, often with boiling points of similar value.

fractionating column the column above the boiling mixture in a fractional distillation experiment.

free electrons the outermost electrons of atoms in a metal crystal that can move easily from atom to atom. The free electrons are responsible for a metal's ability to conduct heat and electricity.

freezing mixture a mixture of ice, water and salt.

Henry's law says that the concentration of gas dissolved in a liquid at a constant temperature is proportional to the partial pressure of a gas. In symbols,

$[gas] / p_{gas} = K_h$

homogeneous means that a every part of a substance is the same as all other parts.

hydrogen bonding the attraction between a hydrogen atom attached to a highly electronegative atom in one molecule and the electronegative atom in another molecule; e.g. HF, H_2O.

ideal gas an imaginary gas in which the molecules have negligible size, no intermolecular forces, and where the collisions are elastic.

ideal gas equation $PV = nRT$

where P is the pressure, V the volume, n the number of moles of gas, R the gas constant, and T the

Kelvin temperature.

ideal solutions solutions that obey Raoult's law.

immiscible liquids liquids that do not mix, but form two layers when put together.

instantaneous dipole forces the forces that occur between molecules when the uneven movement of the electrons causes one part of each molecule briefly to become negatively charged and another part positively charged.

intermolecular forces the name given to the forces that hold, or attract, atoms or molecules together. A common type is induced dipole–induced dipole (van der Waals') forces.

Kelvin scale the temperature scale that runs from zero degrees (0 K), the temperature at which (in theory!) the volume of an ideal gas becomes zero. The Kelvin scale was once called the 'absolute scale'.

kinetic energy energy that an object has owing to its movement.

liquid crystals substances that, although solid, have their molecules arranged in a way that is typical of liquids.

melting point the temperature at which the solid and liquid forms of a substance can exist in equilibrium at a given pressure—normally taken as 100 kPa.

melting point curve that part of a phase diagram that shows how the melting point of a solid changes with pressure.

metastable state a state which is not thermodynamically stable; i.e. one which will change to an energetically more stable state given the opportunity. E.g. a supercooled liquid may not crystallise; but if shaken even very slightly the crystals are made.

miscible liquids liquids that mix in all proportions.

mole fraction the mole fraction, N_A, of a substance, A, in a mixture of A and B is given by

$$N_A = n_A / (n_A + n_B)$$

where n_A and n_B are the number of moles of the two substances.

negative deviations Solutions with negative deviations have lower vapour pressures than predicted from Raoult's law.

non-volatile solute a solute that will not evaporate from a solution.

partial pressure the pressure that a gas (in a mixture of gases) would exert if filled the container on its own. It is given by the equation

$$P_{gas} = N_{gas} / P_{Total}$$

where N_{gas} is the mole fraction of the gas, and P_{Total} is the total pressure of the mixture.

partition coefficient the equilibrium constant that describes the equilibrium that exists for a substance dissolved in two different solvents in contact with each other. In symbols, for a substance A,

$$K_{pc} = [A]_{1st\ solvent} / [A]_{2nd\ solvent}$$

phase the name given to parts, or samples, of a solid, liquid or gas that have the same physical and chemical composition.

phase diagram the diagram that shows the composition of the different phases of a substance that can exist in equilibrium at a series of temperatures and pressures.

positive deviations Solutions with positive deviations have vapour pressures greater than predicted from Raoult's law.

random walk the mathematical description of the movement of molecules undergoing Brownian motion.

Raoult's law says that: the vapour pressure of a solvent in a solution is equal to the vapour pressure of the pure solvent multiplied by its mole fraction in the solution. In symbols this becomes:

$$p_A = N_A \times p_A^\circ$$

reflux the return of the condensed vapour higher in a fractionating column to a position lower on the column (or back into the flask) during distillation.

saturated solution a solution that contains the maximum amount of solute dissolved in it at a given temperature.

solder the common name for an alloy of tin and lead.

solidus the name of the imaginary line at the eutectic temperature running across a phase diagram for a mixture of substances.

solubility the maximum mass of a substance that can exist dissolved in a liquid when the solution is in equilibrium with the solid solute at a given temperature.

solubility curve a graph showing how the solubility of a substance changes with temperature.

solute the substance dissolved in a liquid.

solution a mixture of a liquid containing a solid.

solvated the process in which a solute particle is surrounded by solvent molecules e.g. sodium and chloride ions in water are solvated by water molecules.

solvent the liquid containing a dissolved solid.

solvent extraction the name given to the process of shaking a solution with another immiscible solvent with the aim of extracting the solute from the solution into the solvent.

states of matter the general name given to the solid, liquid, and gaseous forms of all materials.

steam distillation distillation (usually of an organic oil) performed with steam passed into the distillation flask. The presence of the steam lowers the boiling point of the mixture.

sublimation the change direct from a solid to gas (or vice versa).

sublimation curve that part of a phase diagram which shows the temperatures and pressures at which a solid can be in equilibrium with its vapour, but with no liquid present.

supercooling what happens when a liquid is cooled but fails to crystallise at its normal freezing/melting point.

theoretical plates the number of predicted stages required to separate a mixture during fractional distillation.

triple point the combination of temperature and pressure at which the solid, liquid and gaseous forms of a substance can be in equilibrium.

van der Waals' forces another name for the forces between instantaneous dipoles.

vapour pressure the pressure of the vapour above a liquid when the liquid and vapour are in equilibrium at a given temperature.

vapour pressure curve the graph showing how vapour pressure of a liquid varies with temperature. Often the curve is shown as part of a phase diagram.

Index

Terms shown in **bold** also appear in the glossary (see pages 68–70). Pages in *italics* refer to figures and tables.